GREENHOUSE GARDENING FOR BEGINNERS

EASILY START YOUR OWN GREENHOUSE AND GROW FOOD ALL YEAR ROUND

JANET WILSON

ISBN: 978-1-951791-58-2

Get Your Free Checklist:

- Learn How To Build Your Own Tiny House
- Includes Tiny House Plans
- Access to a Private Sustainable Living Community

Visit:

Janetwilson.org

Table of Contents

Introduction

Greenhouse gardening is such an exciting experience, especially if you love growing and nurturing plants. When you set up a greenhouse, you will be able to provide plants with everything they need to grow and thrive. By setting up the most optimal environment, you will help them grow better and you will be rewarded with a beautiful harvest.

As exciting as the idea sounds, there is more to setting up a greenhouse than building a structure and putting plants in it. Have you ever heard the statement, "Anything worth doing is worth doing well?" This statement is a true reflection of the kind of effort you should put into your greenhouse gardening project.

Many people want to experience the joy of having a greenhouse, but they are overwhelmed because they don't know how to start, or they have tried and got discouraged because they couldn't get it right. If that sounds like you, don't despair! This book offers detailed insight into how you can make the most of your greenhouse.

With the information you will find in this book, you will avoid some of the challenges other beginners face when buying or building a greenhouse and then developing, maintaining, and sustaining it long-term.

By implementing the ideas shared in this book, you will master everything from the fundamental concepts of greenhouses and the construction process, to irrigation and how to fight off pests and disease. This book also provides comprehensive details about how to prepare for the growing season and what steps to take for exceptional plant yields.

This book will empower you with all the information you need to get your greenhouse set up right from the start. Whether this is your first greenhouse, or you have tried greenhouse growing and want to do better, or you are an expert wanting to brush up on the fundamentals of success, this book is for you! This book will give you the confidence and skills to get it right because you will learn what to do and how to apply your new knowledge.

This book covers every aspect of the greenhouse experience for beginners and answers many questions common to the greenhouse gardener. Once mastering these basics, you will advance in your success as a greenhouse gardener. As you grow in your skills, you may find that you return to this book often, and still rely on the essential lessons you learned from this book.

Making a commitment to embark on a greenhouse adventure is a serious matter. Most people consider greenhouses as an investment, which they are, due to the cost and effort required to construct and maintain one successfully. However, despite the "seriousness" of the venture, I urge you to relax and have fun while learning. Together, we will make your greenhouse aspirations come true.

Let's begin your greenhouse adventure!

Chapter One:
Fundamental Concepts of Greenhouse Gardening

The primary reason why people struggle with their greenhouse project is that they never took the time to learn about the correct process before getting started. Some of the challenges such people face could have been easily resolved if they had adopted a systematic approach that entails *knowing* before *doing*.

Whether you have tried and failed with a greenhouse project before now or you have never tried to garden in a greenhouse, this book will address the common initial errors and make the process less complicated.

In this chapter, we will lay a solid foundation for developing a greenhouse that will be sustainable in the long term. You will read an overview of what it means to get involved with greenhouse gardening. The ideas and details shared in this section will form the framework through which other concepts will be explored in subsequent chapters.

Greenhouse gardening is for anybody who loves nurturing plants and taking care of them in a specialized environment while enjoying the yields that spring forth. While there are no educational requirements for starting a greenhouse, it is recommended that you learn how to establish your greenhouse correctly from the start.

A greenhouse is a building where plants grow, and the structure can vary in size from small to very large depending on the gardener's needs and choices. As a beginner, you may want to start on a small scale using a modest structure you can easily manage. Greenhouse gardeners who use larger structures are usually experts who have been gardening for a long time; thus, they can handle a more complicated and high maintenance structure.

The first greenhouses date back to the Roman Empire under the rule of Emperor Tiberius. Since then, greenhouses have evolved in their design and uses, and greenhouses have become a common feature of gardening culture.

So, how does a greenhouse work? A greenhouse reduces the rate of thermal energy flow out of its structure, and this happens by impeding the heat absorbed within from leaving its confines.

The material used for greenhouse roofing and sides is usually either glass or plastic. This is because these materials enable the easy penetration of sunlight to the plants. The sun is crucial to warming a greenhouse especially because it heats the soil inside the greenhouse. As it cools in the evening, the warm ground releases heat inside the greenhouse, which provides warmth to the plants in the confined space.

Greenhouses can also be wooden or metal structures that are partially walled-in and covered by plastic or glass sheets. While other materials can be used for greenhouse construction, it is essential that whatever is used allows for light and air to penetrate and circulate. Generally, the building is shaped with four walls, a roof and a single entry/exit area.

In some countries, greenhouses are built to a specified standard and offered for sale to gardeners who do not want to go through the building process. However, as a beginner, if you don't have the financial capacity to buy a greenhouse, you can construct yours just the way you want it. This is easier if you are starting on a small-scale. In Chapter Three, you will find more information on greenhouse construction that you can use as a guide.

Greenhouses safeguard plants from excessive cold, heat, and pests. Greenhouses make it possible to grow various types of crops throughout the year, including fruits, vegetables, and flowers. These types of plants are some of the most popular ones grown in greenhouses.

Since they can be installed anywhere, there are few climate related restrictions on what type of location you need for constructing greenhouses. The highest number of greenhouses are found in high-altitude countries. An excellent example of such a region is Almeria in Spain, where they have greenhouses on over 50,000 acres of land. The reason for this trend in such countries is because they are concerned about maintaining a sustainable food supply, and greenhouses help them meet the demand by extending the growing seasons and allowing greater control on inputs. Since greenhouse gardening makes the extension of the growing season possible, growers can grow certain prized crops that usually can only be found in areas with very long, hot seasons. For example, if you love a particular flower or vegetable and you can only get it in the summer, with a greenhouse, you may be able to enjoy the plant all year round.

Greenhouse gardening is also one of the best ways of staying connected to nature. Most people agree it is a fun and healthy hobby. This idea of enjoying crops all year round is one of the most prominent advantages of greenhouse gardening. The rising cost of food is a phenomenon that affects people in all countries. Think about how relieved you will feel knowing that you grow your own fresh produce. It is an exciting idea to imagine how it will help you cut down on grocery shopping, provide you and your family with plentiful organically grown vegetables. In addition, a greenhouse is an investment that will give you increasing annual returns on your harvested yields, and increase the value of your property.

You can build your greenhouse in various styles. Maybe it will be very utilitarian and made with cheap or reclaimed materials, or maybe it will be fancy using expensive materials and labor. Either way, you have many options for how it will look. In deciding on a location for your greenhouse, however, you must determine the best place for it to reside. Be mindful that while the structure can be based on your preferred style and budget, the site must be ideal. We will discuss more about picking the right location in Chapter Two.

After deciding on a suitable location, you can start building your greenhouse. You will start by selecting and building the size of greenhouse that you want. However, the process doesn't end with building the greenhouse itself. The success of your greenhouse hinges upon the effectiveness of your greenhouse management. The managerial aspect of setting up and maintaining a greenhouse is the most extensive and detailed aspect of your work as a gardener, as it encompasses every aspect of greenhouse gardening.

If you set up a beautiful greenhouse with the finest materials, yet fail to manage it daily, the project will fail. As such, from the start of your greenhouse experience, you must accept that management s time-consuming but rewarding. Most of the successful greenhouses you may know about are operated by committed individuals who learned a lot about greenhouse management and consistently applied what they learned. In subsequent chapters, you will learn various aspects of greenhouse management; from irrigation and pest control to greenhouse cooling systems.

A greenhouse is also a long-term investment that can consistently offer yields so long as it is properly managed. At first, you may have to spend a lot of time trying to understand all that it entails, but when you get used to it, you will realize that it is a continuous process that requires extra space. Therefore, even if you are going to start with a small greenhouse initially, your location should be considerably larger than the structure.

Your location should have enough growing space to make expansion easy when you start to outgrow the initial land inside your greenhouse. You might want to add outdoor gardens, expand the greenhouse or set up additional greenhouses or structures related to gardening. In most instances, greenhouse gardeners always need more land than they initially thought, and if the area around the greenhouse is not enough, they will eventually have a problem.

Even if you don't feel like expanding at the beginning, you should consider that you might want the option later. You will be glad you did because of the many benefits greenhouse gardening offers. Yes, there are financial benefits, such as providing your own food, but most striking are the health-related benefits. Organic plants you grow in your greenhouse are healthier for you than commercially produced food. Furthermore, gardening is a robust physical activity that is also soothing for the mind.

It is a generally known fact that most plants and foods we purchase are grown with the addition of chemicals and preservatives that are known to cause harm to the body. This realization has led to an increased interest in organic greenhouse gardening. More and more households, especially those with kids, are taking intentional steps towards establishing their greenhouses so they can have unlimited access to healthier food.

Aside from being a cost-effective way to produce healthier food, greenhouse gardening also offers tastier and more diverse options for the foods you can grow and eat. This is especially true of vegetables and fruits that you may only get frozen, in cans, in restaurants or specialty shops, or not at all. These crops, when fresh, are even more delicious than what you have ever tasted in canned or frozen foods.

With all of the benefits highlighted thus far, I'm sure you are getting excited at the prospect of learning how to get started with your greenhouse gardening.

At this point you may wonder, "What is the difference between a garden and a greenhouse, and why can't I plant everything in my garden and get the same organic yield?" The most concise answers are:

- A garden is an outdoor environment and a greenhouse is an indoor environment; and,
- A greenhouse gives you immense control over the growing environment, which can result in better yields.

To explain more fully, one important advantage of growing in a greenhouse is the reduced possibility of crops being negatively affected by seasonal weather. When plants are exposed to harsh and irregular weather conditions, it can affect seed germination, vegetative growth, and ultimately the proer ripening of the vegetable or fruit.

Greenhouses enable plants to receive moisture to boost their growth while providing temperature control so plants can grow effectively in an optimum environment. Furthermore, if you were to rely on an outdoor garden, pest control would be much more tasking because the plants are vulnerable to attacks from pests in the broader environment.

Additionally, the length of the growing season is extended with a greenhouse, unlike with outside gardens. Those special vegetables that are seasonal, or have long growing seasons, or really hot temperatures will not grow in all gardens. Greenhouses offer a more comprehensive and advantageous gardening process, and as we continue on this journey, you will discover more reasons why this is true.

Another fundamental concept to consider with greenhouses at the beginner stage is the role of research. I must commend you on getting this book because it is an important part of your research for your greenhouse project. Any beginner who skips the research stage with greenhouse gardening will miss out on a lot of vital information, and consequently, have less success.

The best way to carry out greenhouse research is through books like this that offer detailed insight into what to expect when setting up a greenhouse. Additionally, you can also reach out to other people who own greenhouses to get more information about how it works for them.

If you are keen on making your greenhouse experience an outstanding success, you will make enough time to research. Think about research as your first step, one that gives you a strong foundation to build on. Just like planting a new seed, the process starts humbly, but the seed will grow into a thriving, nourishing plant. A strong foundation of knowledge will lead to success with your greenhouse, as you will be functioning with a complete understanding of how it all works.

Well, there you have it, you have just learned the fundamental concepts of greenhouse gardening. This chapter introduced some of the key ideas that we will expand upon in this book as we build towards really understanding the nature and operation of greenhouses.

In the next chapter, you will learn about the factors to consider when buying a greenhouse.

Chapter Two:
Buying a Greenhouse - Ideas and Factors to Consider

When you decide to buy a greenhouse, you will be faced with a myriad of options and choices that include location, size, design, heating system, etc. In most cases, when people lack a prior understanding of what to expect from greenhouses, they end up feeling overwhelmed by the numerous things they need to do. This chapter's objective is to provide an easy checklist of the ideas and factors to consider when you are ready to buy a greenhouse.

The fact that a building looks good or seems right for a greenhouse doesn't mean it is good enough for a greenhouse. Moreover, some unscrupulous people are able to sell unsuitable buildings as greenhouses because many buyers lack an understanding of what to expect. The checklist below outlines the key considerations to focus on so you can make the right choice.

Location, Location, Location

Regardless of the proposed greenhouse style, it is crucial that the location has adequate exposure to the sun. The sun is vital because its natural UV rays are critical to a plant's growing ability. If your proposed site for the greenhouse doesn't guarantee at least six hours of direct sunlight, even during winter, then you may have to consider purchasing grow lights.

The location of your greenhouse is also essential because it influences every other consideration in the checklist.

Size of the Greenhouse

The size of the greenhouse will also be discussed in Chapter Three when we talk about construction because, just like location, size greatly influences greenhouse purchasing decisions. Specific factors will determine the size of the greenhouse you select, but the most crucial factor of all is what type of plants you want to grow.

While some plants are okay with smaller spaces, some others require a larger area, and if you are going to plant numerous flowers or vegetables, then you might need a bigger greenhouse. Another consideration for size is if you plan to store your gardening tools and supplies in the greenhouse or if you have a separate storage area for them.

If you already know that you are going to eventually expand your greenhouse once you get comfortable with your first one, you might want to get a greenhouse that can be extended or added on to. With an expansion in mind, be sure to buy a greenhouse that can grow to suit your long-term vision.

Watering System

Many gardeners prefer to use a watering hose to water the plants in their greenhouses, and some have no other option but to use a hose. Others may not even have a hose hookup and they water with watering cans or buckets that they have to fill from either an inside or outside water source. If you have no other option, of course, do the best you can! However, you should know, or maybe you already know from experience, that this is not an ideal watering system for several reasons. The most obvious reason is that you may not always get out to the garden to water when it's watering time. This can have disastrous consequences for your garden. You can even lose your entire season of work by forgetting or being late for watering on a really hot day.

As such, you should consider a greenhouse that has an internal watering system, or even irrigation, installed. This will enable the efficient watering of plants on a prescribed schedule. You will learn more about watering systems in Chapter 7 in the section about greenhouse irrigation.

Heating and Cooling Systems

Heating and cooling systems are crucial factors to consider when buying a greenhouse, as it helps maintain an optimum greenhouse temperature. This optimum temperature aids the rapid and healthy growth of plants. If you are paying a lot of money, you should expect it to come with a proper heating and cooling system.

Heating and cooling systems are so vital that they are split into two separate chapters in this book. Before we get there, you should know that one of the best ways of ascertaining if the temperature is correct in the greenhouse is through a thermometer.

The greenhouse should have a pre-installed thermometer to monitor the temperature. Your plants could die in the greenhouse garden without proper heating and cooling systems; as such, never negotiate on the quality of either of these critical systems.

Greenhouse Design and Insulation

Design and insulation are both crucial, especially if you live in a freezing climate with thick ice and snow during the winter. If you are going to grow vegetables all year round, then your greenhouse must be properly insulated.

For such situations, you will require multiple-walled polyethylene, which provides excellent insulation for greenhouses. Some also offer light diffusion due to the opacity. Polyethylene film is a relatively cheap material for greenhouse insulation, however, unlike the other insulation options such as glass, polyethylene film is not durable, and it has a short life span. Polyethylene film may seem easily affordable at first and suitable for any greenhouse budget, but you will have to upgrade it consistently over time.

If you have a bigger budget, you can use tempered glass which will not degrade even after many years of intense sunlight.

Another reason your local climate is crucial when considering the design and insulation of a greenhouse is the wind. Strong winds can pull down weak greenhouse insulation, so if you live in an area prone to high winds or heavy snow, regular polyethylene film will not be ideal. You might need the more robust, thicker, textured polyethylene film.

If you want to use glass in a cold area, consider if it has a heat-retaining glass coating.

We will also talk further about insulation in Chapter Three because it is a vital step in the construction of your greenhouse.

The Strength of the Foundation

Most potential greenhouse buyers focus on everything but the foundation of the greenhouse. Some people assume that because the greenhouse is not a structure with numerous rooms, the foundation doesn't matter. This is untrue! The foundation is essential, especially if you are keen on keeping the greenhouse for a long time.

The kinds of materials used for the foundation will determine its longevity. Many greenhouses are laid with concrete footings, and some others are constructed using wooden posts or frames. Regarding the foundation and the kind of materials you choose, make sure you also consider the engineering regulations in your community. There may be permits required for larger structures with concrete foundations.

Framing and Window Materials

The greenhouse window panels are also a very crucial consideration as you think about the outer layers of the greenhouse. There are three options for greenhouse panels: diffused, semi-diffused and clear. These different options influence the extent of light penetration into the greenhouse, and thus the amount of light the crops will receive.

For this reason, you may want to consider what your growing plans are. If you want to start seedlings to transplant outdoors, you will require brighter light from clear panels that boost the seed's sprouting. You will notice that your plants spring forth faster and are healthier. If you are going to grow plants to maturity, you will need diffused light, as this helps plants gain optimum photosynthesis over the course of their growth. You can always discuss the options with your seller or other installation expert to decide on what might work best for you.

Ascertain the Level of Built-in Pest Control

Since pests are a part of nature's life cycle, you may never have a 100% pest-free environment for your greenhouse. Despite that, you can buy a greenhouse with some insect controls in place such as screens for all open areas, including the doorway, the water systems, and all vents. Simple screens are one of the best ways to control pests in the greenhouse.

Landscape and Logistics

You previously learned that location is the first thing to consider when planning for your greenhouse. If you get it right, you will also take care of many other considerations at the same time. For example, you need to ensure proximity to a water source. At the same time, you need to locate the greenhouse away from falling hazards such as tree branches that may come down in a storm. You need to be able to access it conveniently. A greenhouse can be a beautiful addition to your property, or it can be inconveniently located and thus difficult to maintain. Visualize how it will look, work through how you will use it on a daily basis, and then choose the right spot to set it up.

Regarding logistics, there are various things to consider. During construction, and regularly during the life of your greenhouse, you will want to bring in supplies and take out your harvest. Your location should be conveniently located where you can drive up close enough to load or unload, then use a trolley or wheelbarrow to carry your supplies if needed. When you are harvesting, you will need to bring your harvest out from the greenhouse, and either into your house or your vehicle. For this reason, you don't want to be too far away from your house, road or pathway system.

In some communities, there may be regulations for buildings such as greenhouses if they are of a certain size. If you want a very large, glass walled greenhouse on a concrete foundation with electricity, irrigation and plumbing, you may need to get a permit or follow specific building codes. In some communities, you may have to get permission from your neighbors or community association before installing the greenhouse. Some communities may have fewer or no regulations for smaller greenhouses. This is especially true in rural areas. It is your responsibility to discover these rules before installing your greenhouse. Please make sure that before buying or setting up your greenhouse that you know the relevant rules and refine your plans to ensure that you adhere to them.

Reputation and Service

Even if you are buying the smallest greenhouse, you may spend a lot of money and effort to set it up. It is crucial to check the reputation of the seller(s) and understand the kind of services they offer. Make sure you understand the level of installation, if any, they offer.

You will be helping yourself by learning about the company before making a final purchase. You can start by doing research about the product and the company on the internet. You could also ask the opinion of someone who may have done business with the firm before. You could also get someone you trust to give an honest assessment of the seller and the product you intend to buy. Technology has made fact-checking so much easier, especially if you are trying to look up business reviews on the internet.

Find out if the company offers a warranty. If they do, how many years do they offer and what are the kinds of issues that the warranty covers? Get to know how long they've been in business and how many of these greenhouses they have sold. Ensure you are dealing with a known seller with a proven track record because even if a company offers you an extended warranty, if they aren't in business in a few months, it's your loss.

In addition, you need to know about their services. Do they offer after-sales technical assistance? Are their representatives available during weekends if you encounter an emergency? As you ask these questions, remember to listen carefully to the answers and use the data you gather to make an informed decision about whether to proceed with the purchase.

If you don't use a checklist and ensure that your greenhouse satisfies your most important requirements, you might end up with a unit that is constantly plagued with problems. Sadly, you may have to spend more money trying to renovate and revamp the greenhouse when you discover it isn't right for your gardening purposes or doesn't perform the way you expect.

These comments aren't meant to discourage you! They are meant to inform you so that you can avoid the common mistakes of a beginner and have the best chance at success. As such, when you are ready to make your first greenhouse purchase, please utilize the checklist as a guide.

For some people, buying a greenhouse is the preferred option, however, some others may prefer to construct a greenhouse. Chapter Three offers insight into the greenhouse construction process, so that you can consider which is best for you and make your decision.

Chapter Three:
Building a Greenhouse

If you decide that you want to consider building your greenhouse, you will want to know all the right steps to take, just like when you were learning about buying a greenhouse. In this chapter, we will outline the most important things you need to consider. Although greenhouse construction is much more difficult than just buying one, it is an achievable goal when you know what to do.

Here, we will also expand upon some of the ideas you learned in Chapter Two; however, this time, it will be in the context of your own construction plans. You have to be knowledgeable and hands-on with every stage of the build. This is required for a successful construction experience.

Let's learn how to build a greenhouse!

Step One - Budget

You should absolutely have an idea of how much you can afford to spend before getting started. The amount you spend will depend on the decisions you make. The cost of greenhouse construction will vary based on the kind of design you choose and the kind of infrastructure you implement. This includes the building itself, as well as irrigation, cooling systems, etc.

After reading this chapter, you will know what to expect from the building process. Then you can make some decisions about what type of greenhouse you want, and how much complex equipment you want to run, if any. Price out various components that you want and make decisions from there. Put together a budget that lists out all the costs of the components you are considering. Don't be afraid to make several budgets that represent variations of your plan, so that you can see how different options will affect the final price.

If you only have a specific amount of money, work on your design concept until you are within those budget limits.

Regardless of how much of a budget you decide on, please remember that it is the first and most crucial step when planning for construction. If you don't have your financial plan together, your expenses might get out of control, resulting in a final cost that is way more than expected.

Step Two - Choose a Design

Greenhouse designs are many and varied. They range from simple tents draped in insect mesh that keeps bugs away to fully insulated structures with power and plumbing.

Some of the different greenhouse designs that are available include the barn-style greenhouse, which is inexpensive to construct. There is also the hoop style greenhouse that is very popular with beginners.

While some designs are expensive because of the extravagant style and extensive construction and material costs, some are very affordable and easy to set up. Your preferred greenhouse design should be based on your climate, the kinds of plants you want to grow and your future expansion plans, if any.

As we discussed previously, your budget also influences the kind of design you choose. You may not be able to afford your dream greenhouse, but with a realistic budget in mind, you can find a design to suit your needs.

There are other factors that affect design that you will want to consider before finalizing your decision. These factors are outlined in the steps that follow. Review them, and then come back to your design ideas to incorporate what you have learned.

Step Three - Location

Depending on the land that you have available, you will want to select the ideal location for your greenhouse. Your greenhouse location should be one with access to good and consistent sunlight. The ideal orientation for a greenhouse is facing the sun. If you live in North America, then your greenhouse location should be facing the South or South East. If you live in the Southern hemisphere, your greenhouse direction should be North West. This is ideal because it can get full sunlight all day, but areas with less sun will work depending on what plants you want to grow. As long as you get at least 6 hours a day of sun, your plants should be fine.

In addition, you should pay attention to how the seasons affect the location. Do not settle for a location near evergreen trees that will cast a shadow on the greenhouse and prevent sunlight from streaming in. Similarly, don't place your greenhouse under deciduous trees that will shade the greenhouse, and then drop its leaves all over the greenhouse and any adjoining gardens. Placing the greenhouse on a windy hill will cause undue strain on the structure, and cause breakage to the roofing material. Areas subjected to seasonal flooding should be avoided.

Your greenhouse should have access to electricity, since most greenhouses require heat and ventilation to maintain an optimal temperature. It should also have easy access to a source of water. Your greenhouse is ideally located in fairly close proximity to your home so that you can tend to your plants easily.

Step Four - Covering Materials

Choosing proper coverage for the roof and sides of your greenhouse is crucial for creating a productive growing environment. Your coverings should be sturdy, non-toxic, and durable. They shouldn't tear under harsh weather conditions such as wind or snow.

For a greenhouse covering, you can use various types of plastic film. UV-stabilized polyethylene, which contains BPA's, is very affordable. Non-toxic LDPE grow tarps are also ideal because they last longer. However, plastic films have to be replaced occasionally as PET plastic has a shorter life span than non-toxic LDE plastic.

Another option for roofing and sides is hard double-walled plastic such as multi-wall polycarbonate. Polycarbonate can be curved around the greenhouse frame, it saves up to 30% energy and is also double-walled, making it durable and an excellent insulator. Polycarbonate is also more reliable than glass since glass is so breakable. As such, it can easily chip or crack during construction or at any time due to weather or an accident. Fiberglass is also a great option, since it is very durable.

After deciding on your preferred covering, the next step entails the construction of the greenhouse frame that you will put your chosen covering on.

Step Five - Construct the Frame

The frame of the greenhouse is what holds the structure together, and it needs to be solid and well-constructed. The frame should sit on some kind of foundation or base frame with sturdy reinforcement so that it can withstand the wind. Some greenhouses are built on a full concrete foundation, but some people prefer to plant directly into the soil under their greenhouse.

You will start by marking out the perimeter of the location you have chosen and digging a foundation there. Make sure it is deep enough to take on the weight of the entire greenhouse. Start setting up the frame by using strings and stakes to outline the ground where you want the supports built.

For a hoop house, you can reinforce the structure with rebar pounded or dug into the ground. This should be done every 4 feet while leaving 28 inches protruding from the ground. After setting up the rebar, place 20-foot sections of tubing over the rebar to create the frame. Run another long section of tubing the length of the greenhouse along the inside roof line. Then stretch a non-toxic plastic film over the frame and attach it to the beams at the bottom.

Wooden framed greenhouses also benefit from a foundation or reinforced foundation elements such as concrete piers or metal screw pilings. If you are building a wooden frame greenhouse, you will want to use pressure treated wood. If the wood is untreated, it will degrade after a few years. Learn more about treated wood by asking the attendant at your lumber store.

While framing, you should also decide where you want the greenhouse door. It can be either on the sides or at the front. Having a door on both ends is also an option since it assists with ventilation and humidity control.

Next, you will seal the openings in the roof and sides with plastic, fiberglass, or glass depending what you have chosen for a covering material.

Regardless of what style of greenhouse you build, you will have to decide about the flooring. If you don't have a concrete foundation and/or floor, you can pour gravel evenly on the ground inside the greenhouse, as this will allow for extra drainage. Ensure that you place a sturdy barrier cloth under the gravel, or the weeds will just grow up through it. If you plan to plant directly in the ground, including in raised beds, you will want to prepare your ground inside the same way as you would outside, by turning it well and adding nutrients if needed.

After constructing the frame and covering it, you are almost ready to start growing plants inside your greenhouse. You now have a fully fitted structure in place. For some people and in some climates that do not have extreme weather, you can stop right at this stage and start growing plants. You will have to water by hand, and you may need to place a shade cloth on your greenhouse on really hot days. That being said, if you are starting with a tiny budget, this will get you started.

Step Six - Temperature Control: Cooling and Heating

To optimize your greenhouse experience, and to create the ideal conditions for plants, it is helpful to have a cooling and heating system. These are very important to greenhouse construction. For both cooling and heating systems, you should set up fans to create airflow throughout the greenhouse. The fans should be able to operate fully during winter, so the greenhouse benefits from the circulation of warm air from the heater.

Vents can also be located at the top of the greenhouse for added temperature support and to assist with the correct flow of air and exchange of carbon dioxide. Adjustable vents are useful because you can use them only when needed.

If you are planning to extend your gardening season or even garden all winter, heating is needed for all greenhouses. A steady warm temperature is critical to the success of winter gardening. Rapid cooling of the plants at night can cause a significant decline in plant health, resulting even in crop failure if they are subjected to frost. With the help of a ventilation system, heating systems can circulate warm air around the greenhouse.

Heat sources can include a simple electric heater or a wood or oil-based heater. Each option has its own safety considerations. For electric, they include safe installation and operation, and for wood or oil, they include proper venting outside, and safe storage.

If your greenhouse covering is made of glass, then you can install a forced-air system, which provides the greenhouse with both heating and cooling.

No matter what kind of heating or cooling system you use, don't just install one thermometer to monitor the temperature. Have several of them in case one malfunctions and gives inaccurate readings. Also, having the thermostats in different locations allows you to observe the variations in temperature in different areas of the greenhouse.

Cooling systems utilize mechanical and natural ventilation to bring down the greenhouse temperature. They are vital because a plant that is overheated will die. A good cooling system also makes it more pleasant to work in the greenhouse. Most cooling systems are like large fans that are installed on one of the end walls. Always select an appropriately-sized cooling system that is just right for your greenhouse.

Step Seven - Environmental Control Systems

Environmental control systems are a state-of-the-art way to ensure the integration of cooling and heating systems with other automated functions that optimize your greenhouse operation. Other automated functions might include irrigation systems, dehumidifiers, computers and lights, to mention just a few. Controlling all aspects of the growth environment can ensure the best results with your plants. When these systems are automated, it takes a lot of work out of managing your greenhouse. It also ensures that human error is removed from many of the critical operations. For example, if you go away for a weekend, your plants won't die because you weren't there to water them. Greenhouse gardening is all about your ability to control the planting environment for the benefit of your plants. By being able to guarantee your growing conditions, you are more likely to have a successful harvest.

With environmental controls, select the most energy-efficient control system that you can. If you get the right control system, you will find that they are straightforward to use and a reliable and useful technology for your greenhouse. The biggest downside to these control systems is the cost. These systems can be very costly, and for most small-scale gardeners, they are priced out of budget.

Step Eight - Additional Plans

Additional plans entail other steps you might take after building your greenhouse. Always keep this option open because there are always ways to improve your greenhouse. If you are required to follow specific permit guidelines, make sure that you adhere to all stipulations.

There are many additional considerations. One of the most important is your watering system. It must be reliable and easy to use. Will you be watering manually, or will there be an irrigation system? An irrigation system greatly reduces the work involved in maintaining your plants, but some can be expensive and tricky to set up and maintain. Some are very simple and affordable, so shop around to see what options might work for you. If you plan to water by hand, make sure that you have a hose that is long enough, and that it has a good wand end that you can shut on and off while using.

If you are constructing raised beds inside the greenhouse, you will have to get them built and filled with soil. You can also grow in pots on slatted tables that allow water to drain through but plants in pots require more precise watering. Some people get excellent results by rototilling the ground under the greenhouse, adding soil amendments and then planting directly into the ground.

You should also plan to properly finish the exterior of the greenhouse structure. Check for openings that could become passageways for pests and make sure all fasteners that hold the covering together and on the structure are firmly in place.

Since you will be putting in a lot of effort into this project, it is important that you ascertain the quality of the materials you are considering at all stages of the greenhouse build. Cutting corners on quality will compromise your greenhouse in the future. If you know someone who has already constructed a greenhouse, you can reach out to them about their experience, ask them, what has worked for them, and where they bought their building materials.

Constructing a greenhouse can be a very challenging process for a beginner but it doesn't have to be if you have done your research. Now that you understand some of the fundamental concepts and steps involved, you will be better informed about your options, and you can plan and budget accordingly.

In the next chapter, let's talk about the difference between a greenhouse and a polytunnel house.

Chapter Four:
Difference Between a Greenhouse and a Polytunnel House

One of the primary reasons for the inclusion of this chapter is because many people fail to recognize the difference between a greenhouse and polytunnel. Buyers need to know the difference between a greenhouse and a polytunnel house in order to make a truly informed decision about what kind of structure to get.

Both structures provide a covering for plants that protects them from harsh weather conditions and pests. Both are ideal for extending the growing season. However, there are clear-cut differences between these types of structures, and we will discuss these differences in this chapter.

Before we outline the main differences between them, let's talk about their similarities.

Similarities Between a Greenhouse and a Polytunnel House

Both types of structures are used to extend the growing season. Both options give growers an early start in spring and a longer autumn, such that plants have a longer growing season. This enables you to grow a wide variety of crops.

Both options shield crops from the outside elements such as rain and snow, which gives you control over the moisture levels in the greenhouse. This lessens the chances of destructive diseases and pests. For example, Phytophthora root rot is a common disease that affects plants when excessive rainfall occurs. Both polytunnel and greenhouses protect plants from diseases related to excessive water. They also provide significant protection against animal and insect pests that you may want to keep out of your greenhouse.

Differences Between a Greenhouse and a Polytunnel House

Site Preparation and Construction Details

With polytunnels, there are fewer requirements for site preparation and construction. This makes them an attractive option for beginner greenhouse gardeners. A polytunnel structure can be constructed directly on the ground, even if it is uneven. Furthermore, they don't take too long to set up. The biggest challenge is connecting the polytunnel structure securely to the ground, so that it doesn't blow away in a strong wind.

Greenhouses on the other hand, take a longer time to install, and unlike with polytunnels, they must be placed on a flat and leveled surface that is permanently connected to the structural foundation.

Furthermore, with polytunnels, the ground preparation process doesn't take a lot of time, unlike with a greenhouse, where more precision is needed to prepare the ground for the greenhouse foundation, which is often concrete or gravel.

41

Purchase Price

Although there are expensive, large polytunnels, these structures are generally cheaper than greenhouses. This is because greenhouses are more highly structured than polytunnels, and often have integrated components like plumbing and electricity. Polytunnels offer lower costs per square foot than greenhouses, yet they still offer high yields.

If you have more money to spend, the cost of a greenhouse with integrated components can be worth it if you really want to maximize your greenhouse experience.

Transportability

When you buy a polytunnel, you have the advantage of knowing that you can move it from one spot to another without a lot of difficulty. This is especially true if you are moving it to a location that is close to the original site. They are very lightweight, so with some help, you can just pick it up and move it.

When you buy or build a greenhouse, you will not be able to easily move it, since they are usually constructed in place in conjunction with a foundation. To dismantle it and move it is even more effort than just building a new one.

Ventilation

Ventilation is crucial because it helps to control humidity, air exchange and temperature. Most plants can dry out or freeze if the temperature changes dramatically. Similarly, an excess of humidity can provide the perfect environment for diseases such as powdery mildew. The ventilation process is different in each type of structure. Polytunnels provide better control over air circulation since they often have large doors on both ends. This provides substantial airflow through the tunnels. Furthermore, you can close them up when you need to.

With greenhouse ventilation, the openings on the roof, door and side vents are crucial to ensure the air gets in. Ventilation is greatly assisted by fans.

Lifespan

Greenhouses can last a lifetime. They are generally sturdy structures with strong coverings on all openings. If you use glass for windows and some of the roofing, you may have to replace panels periodically due to breakage, but overall, the structures don't break down. On the other hand, the covers for polytunnels need to be replaced periodically, and they can be damaged by falling branches, or the structure lifted away by the wind if their anchors are not adequate.

Design

Greenhouses have a myriad of designs available for use, and when put together nicely, it can create a stunning display on a landscape. Design is generally related to the intended end use, the number of integrated components and budget.

Polytunnels don't have many design elements as the structures are standardized. They are often called hoop houses and the design is very practical. They come in many sizes and are covered in plastic. They don't always come with ventilation openings or fixed doorways.

Heat Retention and Shading

Both types of structures protect crops from bad weather and create a suitable planting environment. The plastic sheeting used for polytunnels has less heat retention than a constructed greenhouse. Green polytunnel covers allow less light into the polytunnel, which can reduce the overall temperature and transpiration rate of the plants. This can be advantageous for some crops.

Greenhouses in general provide maximum heat retention while still ensuring adequate light transmission through the glass to the plants. This is because the walls are made of stronger material.

Planting Crops

In greenhouses, plants are generally grown in pots on benches that are raised to waist level, whereas polytunnels are usually used to produce crops directly in the soil or in raised beds. That being said, you can plant in any style using a greenhouse, depending on the type of flooring or foundation you use.

This chapter taught you about yet another option you have for greenhouse gardening. Now you know the differences between a greenhouse and a polytunnel house. This book does not advocate for one particular type of growing structure over another. It is up to you to consider all the information and options and decide what works best for you in your situation at this time.

If you have the money and are planning to stay in the same location for an extended period of time, a greenhouse can offer a longer lasting gardening experience than a polytunnel. A polytunnel has its overall advantages for a beginner gardener. You can get a season or two of growing experience, and then decide if you want to invest in a more permanent structure.

Chapter Five:
How to Maximize Airflow and Cooling Systems

Do you recall how growing up, you learned all about planting a seed? You discovered the requirements to make the seed grow, including sun and water. You may have even learned about the importance of temperature for a growing plant. The temperature of the growing space is critical, and if it is too hot or too cold, you can kill your plants.

One of the greatest advantages of greenhouses is that you can regulate the temperature inside them if you know how.

If you are successful at regulating the temperature, your plants will not be vulnerable to extreme weather conditions that will kill them. However, when regulating the temperature, you must consider both the amount of heat needed when it's cold, as well as how to cool off the greenhouse when it's too hot.

At the height of summer, a greenhouse can be excessively stuffy and steamy if it lacks proper cooling systems. The most worrisome aspect of this is the damaging impact of heat on the plants. For example, if you have tomatoes in your greenhouse, and the temperature gets too hot, you will cause heat stress, and this will impact the health of the plant and damage the growing tomatoes.

The ideal is a steady, moderate temperature. This can be done by regulating the cooling and ventilation systems in the greenhouse.

To function most effectively as an ideal growing environment, greenhouses also need the right combination of shade, humidity, and ventilation. This chapter focuses on the importance of maximizing the opportunities for controlling your greenhouse environment using cooling systems. After you learn about cooling systems, the chapter that follows will focus on heat.

Consider the Size of the Greenhouse

Before making a final decision about your cooling system, you must first consider the size of your greenhouse, since this affects the kind of cooling system you need. For example, getting a high horsepower mechanical cooling system for a tiny greenhouse might be overwhelming for the available space. Always ascertain the right fit for any greenhouse components based on the size of your gardening space, and the specific needs it has.

Ventilating Greenhouses

Another great way of cooling your greenhouse is through ventilation. Ventilation provides a good flow of air through vents at the rooftop or the sides. This air movement reduces heat and humidity in the growing space. There are different ways to achieve good ventilation, and we will discuss some of them below.

To successfully ventilate your space, the size of the floor area, roof, and all sides must be considered so air can flow evenly. You must get a sufficient volume of air moving through the space, not just within the space. For example, one roof vent may only assist in cooling a small area. You can get additional ventilation using side vents, and by opening the entrance.

Unless you are expecting frost or a very cool night, such as you get at the beginning and end of the growing season, keep the vents open all the time, including on warm nights. To prevent wildlife and pests, install a screen or net over the door. Some greenhouses come with automatic vent openers already installed.

Shading

Shading is another crucial technique for fighting off heat in the greenhouse, and if you use it wisely, you will achieve the perfect environment in your grow space. Your plants will grow to their full potential when the greenhouse temperature and the intensity of the sun are moderated by shading. Shading paints is a cost-effective way of filtering excessive sunlight and preventing sunburn on your plants.

You can also add layers of paint to the exterior of your building as summer progresses and gets hotter. Shade paint is suitable for most greenhouses. You can also shade your greenhouse using blinds that can be installed either on the interior or exterior of the structure. External blinds filter sunlight even before it passes through the glass and the heat gets trapped inside the greenhouse. The most affordable blinds are sometimes made from mesh or netting.

When the weather is cooler and the sun is not as intense, you can remove the shading material. However, you must be mindful when you take off the blinds because the weather can suddenly change.

Damping

During extreme hot weather conditions, you can keep the plants fresher through the damping technique. Damping is when you wet the greenhouse surfaces such as pathways, hard surfaces, and walls. This raises the humidity inside the greenhouse because as water evaporates, the moisture levels increase in the air, and this helps the plants cope with the heat. One of the other benefits of increasing the humidity in the greenhouse is that many pests cannot thrive in such an environment. On the other hand, high humidity will increase the occurrence of diseases such as powdery mildew.

You may wonder, "How often can I damp my greenhouse?" You can do it daily when the weather is scorching, but it is best done first thing in the morning. This creates an optimal level of humidity throughout the day.

How to Avoid Water Stress in Plants

Plants with steady amounts of water grow better than plants that receive water inconsistently. Thus, being dedicated to your watering routine is crucial to the success of your garden.

When plants are very hot, they transpire. Transpiration is an efficient way that plants keep themselves fresh; through the loss of moisture in the leaf pore (the stomata). This heat loss cools the leaf down on the surface just like when we sweat: imagine if you couldn't sweat?

When moisture is lost, it must be replenished by watering. If the leaf transpires and then has no source of water, when it overheats it cannot sweat and it will start to wilt. To avoid stress in your plants, you need to pay close attention to them to observe signs of heat and water stress. If the plants wilt, become scorched or dry out, it means there is a water problem.

When you become diligent and intentional about keeping your plants properly moist in a greenhouse, you will prevent stress that could result in decreased plant health.

Evaporative Cooling

Evaporative cooling has to do with the evaporation of water from the greenhouse. This is typically done either through recirculating evaporative pad cooling machines or high-pressure fog systems. With evaporative pads, you use mechanical fans that pull the air through a wet pad. As the ambient air passes through the pad, the moisture cools the air.

Evaporative air coolers are self-contained units with evaporative pads and a blower. These units are mostly used in smaller greenhouses and mounted outside the structure. They blow moist air into the greenhouse through an opening on the sidewall.

Another option for evaporative cooling is high-pressure fogging, which is useful for both natural and mechanically ventilated greenhouses.

High-pressure fog is an effective way of cooling and controlling the greenhouse environment as it uses less water than the pad and blower system. This system doesn't only cool the air, it also controls any vapor pressure deficit in the greenhouse.

Mechanical Ventilation

Mechanical ventilation is one of the most sought-after kinds of ventilation for greenhouses because it is easily controlled. With this option, you can get the benefits of natural ventilation and still control the airflow through mechanical means if necessary.

Mechanical ventilation improves airflow by extracting warm air out of the greenhouse and allowing cold air in. To use mechanical ventilation, you need first to consider the size of the greenhouse, as this will dictate how many fans you will need to cool the volume of air inside.

Fans are selected based on the cubic feet per minute they will move air, the fans' static pressure, horsepower rating, and size. After setting up the fans, you can control its cooling rates using a thermostat or an environmental controls system. This degree of

51

control and involvement is essential with mechanical ventilation because you don't want to just leave the fan on without checking that the greenhouse temperature is correct.

Natural Ventilation

This type of ventilation allows for natural air flow and exchange within and outside the greenhouse space. For this kind of cooling system, the greenhouse is designed in such a way that it has multiple vents, making it easier for air to enter and exit the greenhouse.

Properly placed vents maximize the natural airflow through the structure, thus allowing excess heat to exit, enhancing the moisture level, and optimizing the exchange of oxygen and carbon dioxide.

One of the reasons growers struggle with natural ventilation is if they didn't consider it before building their greenhouses. Once a structure is built, it is harder to add ventilation. When designing your greenhouse, consider your cooling and ventilation needs.

Natural ventilation is a great supplement to other cooling systems you may be considering. Natural ventilation is also a great backup if any of your mechanical cooling systems suddenly fail.

Cooling Maintenance

Lastly, you've got to ensure that your cooling equipment is properly managed and maintained for long-term use. Regardless of the cost of cooling equipment, you should take good care of everything to ensure optimal operation and prevent malfunctions. You cannot afford a broken ventilator or cooling system when the weather is scorching. Plants are so vulnerable in the heat that only one day of overheating can cause a full crop failure.

All cooling equipment should be cleaned regularly, monitored, and protected from sudden electrical surges. Keep the units free from algae and keep areas where cooling systems are installed free from weeds.

For evaporative cooling, please make sure the doors to your structure are closed when the fan is operational, so the air properly circulates. If you leave the door open, the fan will be overworked without yielding the right results. Randomly check the cooling systems for changes in performance levels and fix any issues immediately.

Cooling down your greenhouse is a compulsory aspect of effective greenhouse management because regulating the temperatures and protecting your plants from heat and water stress is crucial for a successful growing experience.

There are many options to choose from when considering the purchase and installation of a greenhouse cooling system. When you are ready to buy your cooling equipment consider your specific needs and budget.

There is another aspect to the greenhouse temperature narrative that is just as important as cooling, and that's heat! Yes, just as we need to cool the greenhouse during summer, we also have to ensure that the greenhouse is warm enough during cold seasons, including winter if you will be gardening year-round. We will talk about heating systems in the next chapter.

Chapter Six:
Heating Systems

Now that you understand the importance of a cooling system, let's talk about heating systems, which can also be an essential part of the greenhouse operation. Just as we try to cool the greenhouse when it is hot, we should also ensure that it is warm enough at the beginning and end of the growing seasons, and in winter if needed.

Growers must be intentional about maintaining the right temperature in their greenhouses so the plants can grow bountifully. However, heating a greenhouse in the winter can be challenging, hence the use of mechanical heating systems that enable a balanced temperature to be maintained.

In times past, most growers didn't concern themselves with heat system efficiency or emissions. They only ensured the heat was available without considering its impact on the environment. As interest in climate change increases, growers have started to pay attention to the potential impact of their heating methods. Many greenhouses use fossil fuels such as natural gas, coal, or fuel oil for heat. More environmentally friendly options are powered by electricity.

Heating systems have to be affordable, safe for long-term use, and efficient. All heat sources should be close enough to the plants to support their growing needs while maintaining enough distance to be safe.

Let's consider two major categories of heating systems:

- Central heating
- Heating system replacements

Both categories of products can effectively heat greenhouses, and there are various products within each category. Always consider your needs and budget and then pick what will work best for you.

The First Category: The Central Heating System

With a central heating system, the heat is transferred from a hot water pipe to an object. This is often referred to as "radiant heat." This type of heating system utilizes boilers to heat water or to produce steam, and the boilers can burn fuel like natural gas, coal or fuel oil.

These hot water systems are very efficient for greenhouses, and one of the beneficial by-products of the boiler is CO_2. This gas remains in the greenhouse to help the plants achieve photosynthesis. This technique is not usually practical for a small-scale greenhouse because it requires the installation of expensive hardware.

In this system, the warm water or steam has to be transported through pipes around the greenhouse. This process's efficiency is higher than forced air, which we will discuss soon. The pipes used for this technique can be placed around the greenhouse if it is a stand-alone structure.

The floor of the greenhouse can also be heated with hot water pipes that are placed on the ground under a layer of concrete, sand, soil, or gravel. The heating pipes loop around throughout the entire greenhouse floor surface.

Infrared Radiant Heater

With the infrared radiant heater, heat moves from its source to an object in the greenhouse. The heat is transferred from the pipe to the plants. With this technique, air doesn't move the heat, and air temperature will not actually increase, yet the plant will be warm.

This technique requires an infrared pipe or two pipes that run through the length of the greenhouse. The method also consists of a single burner, or several burners depending on the size of the greenhouse and the pipe. With this method, finned pipes are better than bare pipes because they work best with a larger surface area, thus radiating heat evenly.

The infrared heating system delivers more heat when placed in such a way that it faces the plants and it can cover the entire scope of the greenhouse. The fuel source for this method can either be natural gas or propane, and these low-intensity infrared heaters are safer to use in greenhouses than high-intensity alternatives.

Forced Air Heaters

The forced air heater can be either vented or unvented. With a vented forced air heater, the heat from the combustion is transferred to the air through a heat exchanger. The exhaust gases from the combustion must be delivered outside the greenhouse using a flue pipe. Then the oxygen for the combustion is obtained from the environment outside the greenhouse.

For the second option, the unvented forced air heater, the oxygen is obtained from the inside of the structure. The shortcoming of this system is that the gases from combustion remains inside the greenhouse, as all the heat produced by the heater is maximized to heat the air.

The fuel sources used for forced air heaters are either gas, kerosene, or fuel oil, and the by-products of the combustion include: carbon dioxide, vapor, carbon monoxide, and ethylene. Plants can maximize the use of carbon dioxide to an extent, but the other gases will need to be vented. These heaters can be mounted overhead in the greenhouse or placed on the floor, thus enabling heating from either the top or the bottom.

Forced-air heating units can be placed in different parts of the greenhouse and all units used at the same time. This heating system also requires the use of fans to move the air from the heater to the other side of the greenhouse. A great way of achieving this airflow is by using polyethylene tubes.

The polyethylene tube will be parallel to the length of the greenhouse and its plant rows. The tubes come with ventilation holes so that it distributes heat evenly to the plants. This method of heat distribution is one of the best as it does not only release heat inside the greenhouse; it also ensures that the plants get warmth directly.

Most small greenhouse owners can attest to the viability of this method because smaller greenhouses are more heavily impacted by extreme cold. With one heater and an overhead polyethylene pipe, you can heat a greenhouse.

Moreover, smaller diameter polyethylene tubes can be on the side of the benches, under the plant rows and between them. If you want to move air through the whole greenhouse, you might install a horizontal air flow fan. These fans enable proper air circulation such that there is no stagnant air or high humidity air pockets. This protects the plants from the development of certain diseases caused by excessive heat and stagnant air in the greenhouse.

This heater can be set to automatically turn on and off based on the temperature on the thermostat. Compared to a central heating system, it takes less time to heat the air, which means it gradually provides warmth to the greenhouse as opposed to instant hot air which could overwhelm the plant.

A most striking feature about the forced air heaters is their versatility. These heaters are so versatile that they can be used with any greenhouse regardless of the size. The option to use multiple units in larger greenhouses also makes it one of the most sought-after types of heating system.

The Second Category: The Heating System Replacement

The heating system replacement refers to the replacement of a furnace or boiler when they are no longer safe (when it gets to less than 70% efficiency). The heating system should also be replaced when emissions rise above 10% of the recommended EPA standard.

Professional installers should monitor the design and installation of a new heating replacement system to ensure proper and safe operation.

Condensing Boilers and Heaters

Water vapor is a result of the combustion of gas or oil, and this water vapor, with other products, goes up and is exhausted into the atmosphere. With the condensing boiler, extra heat is incorporated in the gas exhaust system, and this makes the water vapor condense back to liquid.

The condensing boilers are most effective when the return water is cool. Under the right conditions, condensing boilers can guarantee 95% efficiency for your greenhouse. However, you should know that condensing boilers and heaters are more expensive than regular boilers. They are a good option because they reliably offer great results.

Combustion Technology

This technique requires using a conventional burner where fuel is continuously injected under pressure. The method uses a specific fuel-air ratio, and it requires an ignition spark to start the burning process. The advantage of combustion technology is that you get a higher efficiency heating system because of the uniformity of the airflow process.

Heat Storage Buffer Tank

The heat storage buffer tank is an old heating system that has been used since the 1970s as part of a solar system. This method is being used in greenhouses and other spaces where industrial plants are grown. This heating method can be maximized with a big insulated water tank that enables the hot water from the boiler to circulate through a heat exchanger to heat the water in the tank.

At night, when the heat is required, the hot water from the tank circulates through the heat pipes into the greenhouse. This technique allows for the installation of a smaller broiler that can be used during the day and at night. Wood fired boilers also work well with buffer tanks as they absorb the heat from the combustion process and are easy to control just like with fossil fuels.

Controls

Lastly, solid-state controls contribute to greenhouse heating systems. These are accurate heating controls with impactful functions, and water temperature modulation can be added to the boiler system. This system allows for the circulation of lower temperature water through radiation because the greenhouse heat needs to decrease in the daytime as well.

The control system also reduces overheating by saving energy and adjusting the water temperature based on outdoor temperature and weather conditions. This process also helps the grower save fuel in hot weather.

Additionally, you can heat your greenhouse by using wasted hot water from power plants if the plants are close-by. You can also use geothermal heat which entails hot water being pumped from the ground to the surface to heat the greenhouse. Remember that the aim of setting up the heating system is to ensure that you strike a balance in the temperature of your greenhouse.

As such, your monitoring and close observation of the system is crucial to ascertain if the heating method you chose is working well for you.

Can a Greenhouse Become Too Hot for Safety?

You already know how important it is to regulate the temperature in your greenhouse, but can the greenhouse actually become too hot to be safe? The answer is YES! If direct sunlight enters the greenhouse from the south or west excessively, you will most likely be overheating your plants because the intensity of the sun's rays will be too much for them. As such, it is possible for bright sunshine to overheat the greenhouse even during the winter. This is why bigger commercial greenhouses utilize digital controls to open and close vents as the temperature fluctuates. Moreover, in addition to digital controls, you also have to check the health of your plants. This is why greenhouses, both large and small, should have vents that allow the hot air to escape at the top so cold air can come in from the openings below or on the sides.

In addition to being too hot for plants, an overheated greenhouse can be unsafe for you to work in. Prolonged exposure to excessive heat can cause physical distress, including dehydration and sunstroke.

Now that you fully understand the role of heating systems and some of the options you can choose from, let's learn more about water and irrigation. We talked about the role of water briefly in Chapter Five, but now we will discuss it in detail because the availability of consistent water is one of the keys to growing healthy and plentiful yields.

Chapter Seven:
Process of Greenhouse Irrigation

A greenhouse irrigation system is a process that ensures the conservation of water while delivering reliable and consistent amounts of water to your plants, usually on a specific schedule. The system allows water to either gradually drip to the roots of the plants through an installed pipeline or hose, or it waters using the sprinkling technique.

You already understand that water is crucial for the survival of plants in greenhouses, but this doesn't mean you should just pour water randomly on the plants. It also doesn't mean you should water the plants only when you feel like it, or only when you remember to. To ensure the plants don't die from your neglect or inattentiveness, an irrigation system can be installed.

If you recall, you learned that excessive heat and cold air can affect the plants negatively. Similarly, excessive water can harm the plants too. One of the key concepts with greenhouse gardening is balance: everything must be balanced in the right proportion, and this includes water.

An irrigation system dispenses water to the plants using a network of pipes, tubes, valves, and emitters. Greenhouse irrigation that uses pipes or hoses that drip at the soil level is a more controlled and efficient system than the sprinkler style system. Greenhouse irrigation has gained a lot of popularity because it is a proven system that guarantees the correct dispensation of water, which contributes to quality yields.

Despite its level of effectiveness and how simplistic it sounds, there is much to learn about how greenhouse irrigation works, the available types for your greenhouse, and how to get the best out of the experience. In the sections that follow, you will learn all these things. Let's begin with the benefits of a greenhouse irrigation system.

The Benefits of a Greenhouse Irrigation System

It Enables the Conservation of Water

Unlike other watering systems, greenhouse irrigation ensures the conservation of water through reduced evaporation and deep drainage. Overall, these systems use a lower volume of water compared to overhead watering with a water wand and hose, flood or overhead irrigation because sufficient water is efficiently applied only at the base of the plants.

Greenhouse irrigation also protects plants from diseases that spread through water contact with foliage. Drip irrigation systems guarantee even distribution of water, even to those parts of the greenhouse where it is hard to water manually. Since these systems use so much less water, they are very effective in areas where water is in short supply.

It Provides an Efficient Filtration System

Most of the greenhouse irrigation systems you will find have filters that prevent clogging of the emitters by little particles on the flow trail. With newer and more expensive irrigation systems, you may get additional filters, thus providing an extra layer of protection from clogging, which can be a troublesome maintenance aspect of these systems.

Greenhouse Irrigation is Cost-effective

Irrigation systems are an essential part of the greenhouse gardening success plan. Regardless of your budget, you cannot do without them as they increase the chance of success so dramatically. Although a greenhouse irrigation system may seem costly, when you compare the value and convenience it offers, you will realize that it provides long-term value.

How to Choose the Right Greenhouse Irrigation System

There are several vital factors to consider when choosing an irrigation system. These are the reputation of the firms that provide the service, and the specific needs of you and your greenhouse.

Size of Your Greenhouse

Yes, we keep coming back to the size of your greenhouse! That is because it is the most crucial thing that determines what else you can do. You wouldn't need a high-capacity irrigation system for a small greenhouse, would you? If you are unsure what will work, speak with some experts who will explain the different systems and give you a quote.

Location of the Greenhouse

Your greenhouse should be located in close proximity to a water source, since this will facilitate the delivery of water to the irrigation system. If the irrigation system is also automated, then it is likely running on electricity and will also need to be close to a source of power.

Maintenance Requirements

Always consider the maintenance requirements of the irrigation system. Some irrigation systems require intense and consistent maintenance that is time-consuming. If you are already giving a lot of your time and attention to your greenhouse, then using such high-maintenance irrigation systems might not be a problem.

On the other hand, if you are very busy, this might be challenging, especially if you don't have additional help, or don't know much about maintaining equipment. As such, you can either go with a sophisticated system and get help with it or go with a simple system that has less intense maintenance procedures.

Work with an Experienced and Reputable Company

Due to the importance of irrigation in the gardening, farming and greenhouse industries, many companies offer installation and maintenance services. If you are installing a large and complex irrigation system, make sure to work with a reputable, certified company. Greenhouse irrigation system providers have a license and insurance. Don't hesitate to ask for a company's documentation before using their services.

Before using their services, consider the experience and reputation of the manufacturing, installation, and maintenance firm. You can ascertain their experience and reputation by reading through customer reviews and ratings. If you know other greenhouse gardeners who have an irrigation system, find out which company they used and their thoughts on the firm.

If you have a small greenhouse or polytunnel hoop house, and have some technical skills, you can purchase simple irrigation systems online and install and maintain them yourself.

Check for Warranty

A good company that offers a quality irrigation system will always have a reasonable warranty policy for their products and services. A warranty is a sign of a quality company, since you can go back to them to resolve any issues that develop with the irrigation system.

Types of Greenhouse Irrigation Systems

Drip Tubing Irrigation

The drip irrigation system for a greenhouse is similar to outdoor irrigation systems. They entail a drip tube which is used to supply water to each of the plant's roots. Multiple tubes can be attached to a central water supply system and extended outwardly, so every line provides water to a pot, plant or garden area.

After positioning the tubes, an emitter will provide small water sprays on the topsoil. The system can be controlled either manually by turning the water on and off, or it can turn on and off automatically using moisture sensors and timers.

Automatic control systems provide timed drips, thus preventing the excessive watering of plants. The system also protects the plants from bacterial infections because the leaves don't get wet.

With this irrigation system, you can ensure each plant gets water, and you can control the volume of water applied to every plant group.

A drip irrigation system can also be controlled using a tensiometer that can be placed amongst plants to detect moisture.

With a computer program in place, it can turn off the system and turn it on when it reaches the preset moisture levels.

Most growers who grow vegetable crops in beds, pots, and bags use this irrigation method since the customized placement enables efficient watering of plants. The effectiveness of this method is portrayed through a comparison with a standard sprinkler system.

A standard sprinkler system offers 75-85% effectiveness when used in greenhouses, while the drip irrigation system provides 90% effectiveness. A more effective system increases the quality and quantity of crops as well as providing extra protection from inconsistent watering.

Perimeter Irrigation

The perimeter irrigation system is a mix of drip tubing and overhead misting. This system typically serves plants on benches. Pipes are attached to the bench edges, and nozzles are connected at different intervals across the pipe's surface.

After connecting the pipes to the primary water supply system, the nozzle will spray the water directly into the middle part of the bench, thus saturating the plants. Most nozzle sprays are adjustable, which means you can direct the water to about 45-90 degrees as needed to water plants of various sizes.

The Trough System

A trough system is a form of sub-irrigation that utilizes plastic or metal troughs placed on greenhouse benches or supported overhead units. After the troughs are installed, the pots are spaced from one end to another. Then nutrients and water are supplied to the plants through spaghetti-like tubes through gravity feeding.

The liquid is pumped to the high end so it can flow through the base of the pots and then it is collected at the end. The solution returns to the storage tank under the benches or below the ground where it is recycled.

This trough system is efficient because of the fantastic air circulation that happens between the troughs. A trough irrigation system is also less expensive than some other systems, and it can be installed easily regardless of the greenhouse design.

Overhead Misting

An overhead misting irrigation system works effectively in greenhouses that are growing all the same plant species, since the watering will be at a standard height above the plants. With this irrigation style, sprinkler heads that emit a fine misty spray are connected to overhead pipes.

Bigger greenhouses are most suitable for this system because the sprinklers can effectively cover a massive area of the greenhouse at the same time. If you must use this method in a smaller greenhouse, use sprinklers that you can easily control.

71

The disadvantage of this system is the propensity for the overuse of water. You can minimize water wastage by having an automated sprinkler and setting it carefully based on the needs of the plants. Another disadvantage to overhead misting is that some plants do not like to have wet leaves in the hot sun. This is especially true of tomatoes.

Mat Irrigation

Mat irrigation systems offer a consistent water supply to thirsty plants. These systems use a specialized mat that has water supplied to it. You place your plant pots on the mat and the moisture moves from the mat into the soil through the drainage holes in the pot.

This system is similar to a self-watering pot as the soil continuously takes water from the mat until all parts of the plant are evenly moist. As the soil loses water through evaporation the moisture moves from the mat into the plant pot.

With this system, you don't have to worry about the plant getting over or under watered. This system is also cost-effective as you only need the specialized greenhouse mat and access to water.

Water Trays and Saucers

With the water trays and saucers system, water is applied on the surface and collected from trays or saucers placed under the plants. The plates and saucers can vary in size based on the size of the benches or pots. This system reduces runoff by holding on to the water draining from pots and making it available for reuse.

The water trays and saucers method is inexpensive and can be reused. The water it collects can either evaporate or be absorbed by the plants or be recirculated. However, to succeed with this system, you must avoid tight plant spacing which will create poor ventilation and lead to the spread of diseases.

Sub-Irrigation

The sub-irrigation system is also known as the zero-runoff method, and it is an environmentally friendly option that conserves water. This irrigation system is usually installed by growers who are keen on improving their plant quality, production efficiency, and uniformity of growth.

With sub-irrigation systems, water and nutrient solutions are given to the plants at the base of the pots. The plant absorbs the water that is fed from below. It can be used for both plants grown in pots and in soil beds.

Some advantages of sub-irrigation include the containment and recycling of water and nutrients. Benefits also include a 50% decrease in water and fertilizer usage. Your plants will be uniformly watered, and regardless of pot size, the irrigation process can be easily changed. With this sub-irrigation system, the foliage will remain dry, while plant growth is assured, and labor input is reduced.

Even when your greenhouse has the best climate control system in place and you are using productive growing methods, if your watering system is not efficient, you won't get good yields. To enjoy beautiful plants, get consistent crop yields and a rewarding greenhouse experience, you must install an adequate irrigation system.

Some growers try to cut corners and costs by sticking to only the bare necessities of watering, which entails using a watering can or a hose. While the traditional watering can or hose will work, you might want to reconsider using them because greenhouse irrigation helps you save time and is safer for your plants since it will guarantee consistent watering. Furthermore, with greenhouse irrigation you can conserve a lot of water.

Now that you know everything about setting up your greenhouse, including construction, temperature control and irrigation, you can get to the fun part; GROWING PLANTS! The next chapter highlights greenhouse growing methods and how you can maximize them for increased yields.

Chapter Eight:
Greenhouse Growing Methods

In addition to everything you've learned thus far, you now need to learn about the plant growing process. If you put a lot of effort into setting up your greenhouse or polytunnel without paying attention to the best ways to grow plants, your overall success will be low.

While you already know the main factors to consider with greenhouse gardening are light, ventilation, temperature and water, there are many fundamental greenhouse growing techniques that you should learn.

You will learn about what you need to get started, the factors that contribute to healthy growth and various growing methods. Although there are many types of growing methods for greenhouses, you are not expected to use every one of them in your greenhouse. Consider what might work best for the kind of plants in your greenhouse and try it. If it doesn't work well for you, next time you can try a different method.

By now, you probably have an idea of what kind of plants you will grow, and you may have researched what their growing habits are. This will help you to decide what may be best for you as you learn more about things like soil, fertilizers and different styles of gardening.

Soil

Many people start with healthy, sterilized soil that comes in bags. Unsterilized soils usually contain weeds and bugs. If you must, bake the earth in the oven for an hour at 250 degrees F to be sure it is sterile. After baking it, add a tablespoon of fertilizer to every gallon of soil and mix it well.

Alternatively, and especially if you are growing organically, you can make your own soil mixtures. If you are gardening a large area and planting directly into the ground, you may want to acquire and add additional screened topsoil or compost to your existing soil.

Seeds or Starters

You can get seeds from your previous plants or buy them from a plant nursery or other store. Starter plants can also be purchased at a plant nursery. Seeds are much cheaper than starter plants, but they take a lot of dedication and patience to grow. Starter plants, while more expensive, give you a guarantee of a good head start on your growing season.

Containers

The containers you use should also be sterilized. To sterilize the container, you can use one part of bleach in ten parts of water, or half water and vinegar, or hot water and good soap. Rinse thoroughly with warm water and allow the container to get dry before using it. You will need pots that are large enough for the plant when it is at its largest. If you start in a small pot, plan to transplant to a larger pot later. Note that you can damage your plant while transplanting, so it is best to only do it once. For example, when you get your starter plants, you will transplant them into a large pot or directly into the ground for the rest of their growing cycle.

Fertilizers

Whether you choose to grow organically or not, plants need fertilizer. They need just the right amount, and you have to be careful not to over or underfeed your plants. Underfeeding results in malnourished plants, but overfeeding can burn the plant, cause damage to its roots and change the soil pH.

If you bought the soil in bags, you may find that it already has fertilizers in them. Check the label carefully. Depending how much fertilizer is in them, you may still need to add fertilizer later in the season. If the soil doesn't contain fertilizers, you will be able to purchase one that suits your needs. Use fertilizers according to directions to ensure optimal growth.

What are the Factors that Affect Plant Growth in Greenhouses?

Humidity

Although rainforests with high humidity are excellent for some plants, it can hinder plant growth for others. The humidity levels should be no more than 70-80%, especially during high-growth periods. Too much moisture can make plants weak and encourage fungal diseases. You can always reduce humidity levels through venting or exhausting the humid air. To increase it, you can spray water on the inside of the structure or on the plants. Moisture levels can also be increased by placing water containers in the greenhouse which will evaporate to maintain humidity levels.

Watering

Except for scorching summer months, plants are watered daily. When very hot, check plants regularly and water as needed. Using well water is best since it is untreated. If you are using city water, always check for chlorine in the water as too much chlorine can affect plant health. If you need to, you can get anti-chlorine drops from a local pet, pool or hot tub store.

For further information, please refer to Chapter Seven about irrigation, as it provides a detailed guide on how to use water properly to boost your greenhouse yields.

Ventilation

As you now know, ventilation is one of the most crucial aspects of growing plants successfully in a greenhouse. Please refer to Chapters Five, Six and Seven which extensively cover how to keep your greenhouse properly ventilated in all weather conditions.

Light

As we have previously discussed, full sunlight in your greenhouse is often ideal, as this will help you cut down on additional heat sources and provide a long growing day. Depending on the needs of your plants and the time of year, plants will need about 6-12 hours of light every day. You can also provide shade to limit the sunshine if it is too intense and add artificial light if you need more light at the beginning and end of the season.

Types of Greenhouse Growing Methods

The Shelf Unit

The shelf unit method is versatile and exciting to use as the spacing between the shelves can be adjusted as the plants grow, or to accommodate various kinds of pots. The shelf method allows you to essentially stack the plants vertically in neat rows. It is easy to use greenhouse irrigation with shelf units. These are most effective with shorter plants like lettuces.

The Grow Bag

If you do not have a lot of space in your greenhouse, then the grow bag method is ideal. This method is also productive for poor soil or garden conditions since you are bringing in the soil and growing above ground. Furthermore, it can be less expensive than using pots. In fact, it is one of the most affordable ways to garden. They are also less breakable than regular pots. Furthermore, you can grow various types of plants in these bags, including tomatoes, cucumbers, okra, flowers, etc. The bags vary in size so you can get different sizes for plants that have different final sizes.

Hydroponic Ebb and Flow Method

With this hydroponic method, you can grow plants without soil using a reservoir located below the grow tank. Liquid nutrients are added to the water, which is pumped into the grow tank and then recirculated back into the reservoir, then used again by the plants. Since it is a recirculating process, this process conserves a lot of water.

Hydroponic Deep-Water Culture

This technique is a hydroponic method where the water flows through the grow tanks to the reservoir. Then the plants float on rafts on top of the water with the roots hanging into the water. This method is mostly used by experts who have a lot of experience since balancing the nutrients can be tricky.

Tower Garden

The tower gardening technique is a vertical form of growing that works for a large variety of plants. With the standard tower garden, you can grow veggies such as spinach, all kinds of herbs and microgreens. You can also have multiple planting cages around the central tower to grow larger vegetables such as tomatoes and eggplants.

Hydroponic Nutrient Film Technique

The nutrient film technique is a hydroponic system that enables growth in small shallow inclined tanks instead of a large container. These gutter-like structures then have nutrient enhanced water passed through. This method is great for plants like mustards, spinach, broccoli, and kale.

Farm Wall

The farm wall growing system is sometimes called the gutter system, and it is placed vertically against a wall. This method is excellent for crops that don't grow into very big plants, such as lettuce, spinach, arugula, etc. Water is pumped from the bottom to the plants in the wall mounted containers.

Raised Beds

Using raised beds is a tried and true method to grow high yields in both greenhouses and polytunnel hoop houses. These are large long boxes that are filled with dirt, usually placed against the sides of the structure. Plants are then grown directly in the deep soil. A pathway system runs between them, often down the middle of the structure, to facilitate access and watering. This is one of the most affordable and simplest methods.

Directly in the Ground

This is the most traditional and simplest way to grow plants. If you have good soil, and very few resources, don't be afraid to just till the soil and plant your plants. This is especially easy if you have a polytunnel hoop house. Let's discuss it further below.

Should I Use Containers or Grow My Plants in the Ground?

Growing plants in the ground has always been a traditional planting method for greenhouse gardening. Plants are usually planted on the two sides with a walkway in-between. Some people cover the walkway with gravel, concrete slabs, straw or wood chips to make walking easier and to keep the pathway clear.

While some gardeners prefer planting in the ground, others prefer using pots of various types. Due to the cost and availability of pots, and the need to acquire soil to fill them, many growers prefer planting in the ground. If you are growing your own food, you may prefer to plant in the ground. If you are planning to sell your plants, it will be easier if they are grown in pots.

Your decision to grow your plants either in the ground or in pots is also dependent on the planting space you have and the type of soil you have. There are pros and cons to each option, which we will outline next.

The Advantages of Growing Plants in Pots

There is a Lesser Risk of Soil-Borne Diseases

With pots, your plants are not overly exposed to the diseases and pests and pathogens that can build up in the soil and infect plants. With pots, you can use sterilized or high-quality soil.

With Pots, You Have Different Options

When you plant in pots, you have a variety of options to pick from; wood, clay, plastic, fiberglass, etc. These options also come in different colors and styles, and you can decorate the pots to suit your preference.

- **Clay pots:** Clay pots are more traditional. They are less likely to topple over since they are heavier. They are also porous, thus protect plants from excessive watering.

- **Plastic pots:** Plastic pots are less likely to break if dropped, but you will need to water the plants in them more often.
- **Wooden pots:** Wooden pots tend to be larger and more decorative. They are also water-resistant with a long-life span.
- **Fiberglass pots:** The primary advantage with fiberglass pots is the fact that they are very durable, lightweight and weather resistant. They rarely splinter, crack, or fade when exposed to harsh weather conditions.
- **Peat pots:** These are great to start seeds in before transferring to the garden or a bigger pot. Peat pots are biodegradable, so you can plant them into the soil without affecting the roots.
- **Polythene sleeve pots:** These are very cheap, and they are easy to store after use.

The Disadvantages of Growing Plants in Pots

<u>*Regular Fertilizer Addition*</u>

Commercial potting mixtures have varying amounts of nutrients, and some have no nutrients at all. As such, you will likely have to spend money on fertilizers. You have to add fertilizers more frequently when you use pots compared to when you plant directly into the ground.

Containers Heat Up and Cool Down Too Quickly

Fluctuations in temperature affect plants in pots faster than those in the ground. If you don't pay close attention to the plants, sudden changes in temperature can lead to damage to your plants.

There is Limited Space to Grow in Pots

While you can keep some flowers, vegetables and shrubs in pots, most types of plants do best if they grow directly in the ground. This is because the roots can expand fully, which results in bigger plants with higher yields. If the plants get really big, they will get root bound, which is when there is no further room for the roots to expand.

Plants in Pots Require Frequent Watering

Containers generally cannot retain water for a longer period, unlike planting in the ground where the water evaporates at a slower rate. If you use mostly small clay pots, you'll find that your plants may dry out faster and you will need to water frequently.

The Advantages of Growing Plants in the Ground

It is Less Expensive

Planting in the ground is less expensive than using pots because you don't have to buy soil or pots and you use less fertilizer. If you have good soil that is loamy and nutrient rich, you can plant directly into the ground. All you have to do is till, plant and water. You may want to add some organic compost or other fertilizer later in the season if you want to increase the nutrients available to your plants.

Makes Watering Easier

When planting in the ground, it is easier to water the plants, since you don't have to be careful about getting the water only into the pots. Loamy soil can hold water and nutrients for longer in open soil than it can when it is in a pot. This means that you will use less water and are less likely to overwater your plants. If you are considering an irrigation system, it is easier to install on a flat ground surface than in pots.

There is No Need to Repot

The process of repotting is often done when the plants get too big for their existing pots. This is time-consuming, especially if you grow numerous plants. It also increases the chance of damage to the plants. Many growers plant their seeds or starter plants directly in the ground in order to avoid transplanting later after the seeds sprout.

The Disadvantages of Growing Plants in the Ground

Disturbances from Pests and Diseases

Plants grown directly in the ground are more susceptible to pests and diseases, and this is a significant drawback. Fungi, bacteria, and other plant diseases spread faster on the ground than in pots. If the soil in a pot is contaminated, out of balance or contains bugs, you can remove the pot and plant that has been impacted so that it doesn't infect other plants. This is harder to do if you plant directly into compromised soil, since it is likely to infect a large portion, if not all of your plants.

Low Soil Temperature

Many greenhouse growers forget to test the soil temperature before planting. Remember that temperature is crucial for successful greenhouse gardening. If the earth is too hot or too cold, you will have little success. If planting directly in the ground, you have to wait until the soil is warm enough before planting, unlike with pots where you can place the pot on a heated pad or cool it down in a cooler before planting.

Soil May Become "Crop Sick"

If you grow the same crops in the same location every year, the soil may become what's known as "crop sick". You will start to notice the plant struggling with diseases while its yields reduce. This is because of the accumulation or depletion of nutrients in the soil that a particular plant uses preferentially. The solution to this problem is crop rotation, letting the land lay fallow for a season, or the replacement of the soil.

Now that you know more about both planting directly in the ground and in pots, you will agree that both methods have strengths and weaknesses. As such, you have to decide what to use based on the factors that apply to your situation. For example, if your greenhouse is in an area with poor soil, you will need to work with pots. If you have good soil and a low budget, planting directly into the soil can be the better option.

The greenhouse growing method you choose is one of the most exciting decisions you will make since it will dictate your gardening routine. Choose the method that you think will be most successful. Regardless of what you plant in your greenhouse, you desire exceptional yields, since you have made a significant investment of time, money and energy. Your crop harvest will be the return on your investment in the project.

After going through this challenging process of setting up your greenhouse and getting things growing, it is only right that you are able to protect and secure this investment. The next chapter provides insight into how you can protect your greenhouse from both natural and human-made issues.

Chapter Nine:
How to Protect Your Greenhouse and Keep It Secure Long-Term

Since you have made such an investment of time, money and energy, you will want to protect all you have worked so hard to achieve. There can be different threats to a greenhouse, both natural and caused by humans. Natural threats are often most worrisome because they can happen without warning, unlike issues caused by human neglect, which are usually preventable.

For example, the weather can change suddenly from a calm day to a strong disruptive windy day that shakes the entire greenhouse to its foundation. In other cases, there may be an extreme cold or heat event, or a pest issue.

This chapter will focus on how you can protect your greenhouse so that you can enjoy the long-term returns of your investment.

How To Protect Your Greenhouse From Heat Waves

Heat can cause a lot of damage to your greenhouse and the plants within it. Mulch can be used to protect your plants in hot conditions. Mulch is a plant saver that reduces heat, maintenance costs, helps you save water, reduces evaporation, and generally protects the plant.

You can use mulch to protect the roots of plants from the outside by placing it around the bottom of the plant or pot. For mulch, you can use materials such as straw, black plastic sheeting or newspapers.

Another way of protecting your greenhouse from excessive heat waves is to adhere to an early morning watering routine. This ensures that the plants have sufficient water, especially at the root zone, throughout the day. Heat stress in a plant is like your skin getting sunburned, and when this happens to plants, they can become brittle and cannot fight off the impact of the heat. In very high heat, check and water your plants several times a day. Carry out light watering if the heat increases throughout the day.

If you use plastic covering and other materials aside from glass, they may become weaker because of harsh weather conditions. As such, you will have to protect the coverings to ensure sufficient protection to the plants.

You can use shading to protect both the covering and the plants inside. Place extra layers of shade or other coverings over the greenhouse when the weather is scorching hot. At night when it cools off, you can remove the additional coverings to allow in the cool evening air.

If you can avoid it, don't plant crops in hot weather conditions. Some very healthy and older plants can survive the heat, but new plants will not survive.

Ventilation and cooling systems are the best way for your plants to survive a heat wave. If you have chosen to install these key pieces of equipment, you will be happy you did when a heat wave comes.

How to Protect Your Greenhouse from Excessive Cold

It is very important to keep your young and tender plants safe from cold temperatures. In fact, excessive cold does a lot of damage to greenhouse plants, and if it is not managed correctly, it can lead to a complete wipeout of your crop.

Supplying heat during extreme cold weather protects your plants from frost. If your greenhouse covering is made of plastic, then you can add additional layers of plastic inside and outside the structure. The extra layer outside keeps some of the harsh cold from entering the greenhouse, while the extra layer inside provides additional protection to the plants from any cold waves that try to enter.

You can use protective measures like cold frames. These are small transparent boxes that you put over the plants. You can purchase them from stores that sell greenhouse equipment, or you can build them with wood and window frames or plastic. The cold frames help to keep the plants safe from the cold. This is especially helpful if the cold frames are within the greenhouse. On sunny days you can keep the lid open to prevent overheating. You can also use cloches, which are like small hoop houses that protect your crops from frost.

As a preventive measure, you can apply a mulch layer at the bottom of the plants because mulch acts as an insulator that holds heat and moisture in the plant during cold weather. You can also throw an old sheet, light tarp or frost plastic over tender plants during cold nights, using sticks to keep the sheets off the plants. Take off the tarp in the daytime so the plants can get air and light.

You can also make deep raised beds for your plants. These raised beds, when filled with dark soil, keep plants warmer than if they are in a flatbed or pot.

Another way of protecting your greenhouse plants during freezing periods is to place a large container filled with water inside the greenhouse. The water will absorb heat from the sun during the day, then at night, the water releases warm air throughout the night.

The best way to protect your greenhouse and plants from the cold is to have a heating system installed. You may have thought about one already, and it is a really great idea if you live in a cold climate and want to garden year-round.

How to Protect Your Greenhouse from High Winds

Greenhouses should be protected from the wind because it can be unpredictable and dangerous. There is no way to make your greenhouse 100% windproof, but you can reduce the level of exposure your greenhouse faces during windy times.

First, make sure the greenhouse is leveled, and the base is securely fixed to the ground. This will keep the greenhouse stable during strong winds. Also, make sure that there are no vulnerable areas in the greenhouse through which wind can get in.

If your greenhouse is made of glass, check for cracks on the panes and replace the cracked glass. Do not take out glass and leave the place open. If a storm is coming, make sure all windows and doors are closed tightly and consider covering them with a layer of wood or plastic.

Try to erect your greenhouse in a location with natural protection from strong winds. Consider using a wind barrier around your greenhouse if the winds happen frequently. If you have trees around your greenhouse, then make sure they are in good condition to prevent the trees from falling on your greenhouse during high winds.

When a storm is imminent, keep your greenhouse area free from items that could be swept up by the wind and cause damage to the greenhouse. This includes lawn chairs, planting tools, etc.

After an extreme windstorm, check the greenhouse for any damage. If you find any, fix it immediately. Never try to repair the greenhouse while a storm is ongoing, since this can be very dangerous.

How To Protect Your Greenhouse From Threats Caused by Humans

A lot of damage is caused by gardeners accidentally or because of negligence. If you are going to keep your greenhouse and plants safe, you must take extra good care of them and be intentional about protecting your planting space.

Consistent System Maintenance

All systems should be maintained appropriately, especially when they are consistently and regularly used. For example, you will use the cooling system more during summer than in the winter, and the heating system more in the winter. Thus, you must ensure that you consistently maintain your systems in the off season, so when you need them, they are ready for use.

Checking the Stability of the Structure

Your greenhouse will be solid and firm in the first few months after construction, but this may not still be true after a strong storm, or a couple of years of use. As you plant more crops and install more systems, the building will take on more weight and require more maintenance and monitoring. There are also more things that can go wrong.

Most greenhouses that collapse during heavy rain or very windy days are already weak and have been left unchecked or poorly maintained. Be sure to carry out building inspections regularly to ascertain the sturdiness of your greenhouse.

Watching the Plants

Another way to avoid a disaster of your own making is by carefully watching the plants for early signs of trouble. Long before a full-blown plant issue arises, there are usually signs of it emerging. For example, if you monitor the plants regularly, you can spot a crop that starts to wither slightly and make adjustments before it withers away wholly.

Watching your plants also helps you know if you need to transplant them to prevent damage to the roots. Observe the coloring of your plants. If you notice changes in the color of the leaves, then it could be a sign of a problem with nutrients.

Protecting the safety of your greenhouse and the plants inside it is a normal part of the greenhouse gardening process. Being proactive with your maintenance and by using close observation, you can prepare for most potential future risks. Although there are solutions for every impending danger, try to prevent issues before they happen. If something does go wrong for you, don't worry! You can handle it! In the very worst-case scenario, you can replant your garden!

Next, let's talk about the growing process itself and go over the steps to take when you are ready to grow plants in your greenhouse.

Chapter Ten:
Preparing for The Growing Season

The growing season is the most exciting time of year for greenhouse growers because it is time to plant and enjoy the fruits of our labor. With the right approach to greenhouse gardening, you can expect exceptional yields. Since the success of your greenhouse is about the right balance of many components, you cannot merely get seeds and put them in the soil when you want to plant. You have to stick to a prescribed growing pattern that is specific to the crops you want to grow.

For example, you will prepare differently when you plan to plant flowers compared to when you plant vegetables. Knowing the differences in growing methods will help you do things the right way, which increases productivity. Although the actual planting stage is relatively straightforward, there is much to learn about preparation before you plant.

Adequate preparation is a big part of getting it right with the seeds, soil, temperature, planting tools, and everything else you will need to grow healthy plants. Healthy plants are the goal for all greenhouse growers because healthy plants give the best yields.

In this chapter, we are going to focus on how to prepare for the growing season by highlighting some of the steps you can take to get your greenhouse ready for planting.

Step One - Declutter the Greenhouse

The first step to take in preparing your greenhouse for planting is decluttering. Sowing and planting in a disorganized greenhouse makes it harder to get things done. In some cases, it will put the plants at risk because a cluttered space is a breeding ground for parasites and disease.

- Take pots, seed trays, compost bags, workbenches, shelves and everything else outside. Throw out or repair any broken items.
- Dead plants and leaves should be removed since these can be home to diseases that will infect the new plants if they remain in the greenhouse. Most people burn the material or compost it.
- Inspect the floor and get rid of pests such as slugs and snails.

Once everything is outside, reassess your supplies to see if you have everything you need. Not everything needs to be kept inside the greenhouse. If you have extra pots or extra tools, you can keep them in separate storage to create space inside the greenhouse.

Get rid of all leftover dirt and unwanted tools from the construction process. You want your greenhouse to be as neat as possible so you can work effortlessly inside it.

Step Two - Clean, Clean, Clean

Now that you have decluttered your greenhouse space, the next step is cleaning. This is the most important step you will take during your greenhouse set up. Cleaning the greenhouse provides a sanitary growing space for your plants and helps you mentally prepare for the planting season.

Start by cleaning on a day that is warm enough for the cleaning water to dry quickly. First, clean the floors by sweeping the entire greenhouse while paying special attention to places pests might linger and hide. Thoroughly sweep all corners of the greenhouse, and if it is too dusty, sprinkle some water on the floor. After sweeping, mop the floor with soapy water and rinse.

Scrub the coverings, whether they are glass or plastic, to remove any leftover debris or algae that may have built up on the glass. This step is crucial because if the glass remains dirty, it will limit the amount of sunlight the plants will get.

Disinfection is next. Disinfect everything from pots to planters, shelves, hose nozzles, benches, and all gardening tools. You can clean them by using hot soapy water or an eco-friendly disinfectant. Always ensure that you wash your tools thoroughly, rinse them, and allow to dry. You should also disinfect the floor to keep it free from bacteria. After washing and cleaning, remember to let everything dry as you don't want to use tools or the greenhouse itself when it is wet. This may take a day or two. Open up the vents and door to ensure good air flow.

Step Three - Prepare the Soil for Planting

Next, you have to check the soil for planting. Depending on how you want to grow your plants; beds, pots, in-ground, or grow bags, you must check that the soil is ready to be used for planting. The soil should be sterile and free of debris. Check for soil temperature because it needs to be warm to optimize the growth of seeds and small plants. Fill your pots or growing beds and spread the soil evenly. Add any fertilizer, nutrients or compost and mix it in thoroughly.

Step Four - Check the Coverings

Your greenhouse covering is the shield that keeps the planting space safe. It should be kept well maintained as well. You already cleaned the covering in Step 2, so now you will check that all coverings are secure with no cracks in the glass or tears in the plastic. If there is damage, fix it before planting begins. Everything is easier to fix when the greenhouse is empty. Failure to keep the coverings in good repair makes it easy for wind, debris and pests to get in.

Step Five - Clean the Water Catchment System

This is a special cleaning task. The greenhouse water catchment system should also be kept clean by removing all leaves and debris from rain gutters installed inside or outside the greenhouse. Check that there are no blockages in the water flow of the pipes, as this will impact how effectively you can water your plants. If there is algae or grime visible, wash it off with a light bleach solution.

If you have various new water systems in place for greenhouse watering, don't assume that because they are new, they are working well. Ascertain the extent of their effectiveness by testing everything.

Step Six - Check the Water Sources

Plants in the greenhouse always require more water than the ones outside. As such, much emphasis is placed on the watering system when preparing for the growing season.

Arrange for extra water storage that will be available when the weather is really hot. Having a 40-gallon rain barrel filled with water is an excellent idea to ensure that if your central water system fails, or you have a general water shortage, you have a backup source of water. A rain barrel is also a great way to conserve water.

If you have an irrigation system, check the components carefully to ensure they work. Test everything to make sure water comes out of all the nozzles.

Step Seven - Reassess the Vents

We have stressed the importance of ventilation repeatedly, and even as you prepare to plant, please note that you must check that your vents are working right from the start. Don't wait until you have finished planting your seedlings or starters before setting up or fixing the ventilation system.

The ventilation systems and outlets should be ready so that you can open all the vents to let fresh air into the greenhouse right from the start. This will optimize your working environment, as well as being best for the plants. After opening the vents, leave them that way for a long time until the greenhouse is cold again at night.

Step Eight - Shading

You have already learned about the importance of shading, so make sure it is ready to use when you need it. If you are starting in the spring, you will not use the shade cloth, but during the hot summer season, or if a heat wave comes, you need to be able to deploy it quickly and reliably. Excessive heat and direct sun can kill your plants, don't underestimate the importance of having your shading plans in place and your supplies at the ready.

Check that your shading cloth has no rips in it, and that no insects or pests have been using it for nesting. Clean it and repair any damage. Fold it up or roll it up neatly and put it away until you need it.

Step Nine - Check the Heating and Cooling Systems

Next, you must check if the heating and cooling system is functional. These should be installed or maintained at the beginning of the season. Since you are planning to grow your crops all year long, you will need these in place before any planting commences. Check to make sure that all sensors and thermostats are functioning.

Before planting, if it has been cold, heat the greenhouse to a comfortable working temperature. This will create a perfect environment to start planting in.

Step Ten - The Exterior of the Greenhouse

Lastly, you also have to prepare the exterior of the greenhouse for planting season. Most growers focus solely on the interior, and the planting process itself, forgetting that if the exterior is not adequately taken care of, they will have issues.

For example, if the greenhouse is very clean and organized inside but the external parts are filled with pests, over time, the pests will get inside. Similarly, if there is damage to exterior panels, pests will come in.

Give some attention to the exterior. Is there dirt and debris around the greenhouse? Do you need to clean the area? What about the trees around the greenhouse, are they sturdy? Is your pathway to the greenhouse clear and safe? Are the plants outside and around the greenhouse pest and disease-free? Check the state of your electrical and plumbing connections and do any required maintenance.

Preparing for planting season is a lot of hard work, but if you take care of the basics we've discussed, and do the right things, you will have tremendous success. As a beginner, your first season of preparation will be the most time consuming, but you will get used to it and enjoy the process every year. Even expert greenhouse growers had the same beginner challenges, and today they look forward to the planting season and every part of the process.

Pests, bacteria and disease are words no greenhouse grower wants to hear, but unfortunately, it is an inevitable part of the growing experience. Nature has to complete its life cycle, and pests and disease are a part of that cycle. In the next chapter, you will learn how to handle them and manage the level of exposure your greenhouse has to such natural threats.

Chapter Eleven:
How to Handle Disease and Pest Control

When setting up your greenhouse and growing your plants, there are some things you have control over and some things you do not have control over. For example, you have control over the watering, and you can even set up an automated system that helps you water the plants at designated times. However, you do not have control over nature; hence, you may have to seek ways to manage it.

Wherever you see plants, you will find pests, but this doesn't mean that you should give up and allow them to ravage your plants. Even if you cannot control the situation 100% in terms of permanently keeping them away, you can manage the situation through effective pest and disease control.

Diseases and pests make your plants vulnerable and will even kill them if they are not kept under control. Pest and disease control is crucial to stay on top of, and there can be cycles that repeat. Even if you fumigate your greenhouse at the start of the planting season it doesn't mean it is safe for the rest of the year.

Pest control is a continuous effort, and it is something you must become intentional about because it determines the success of your plants. You may have some issues keeping the pests away if your greenhouse is located in a pest-infested area. This is why keeping the inside of your greenhouse under control is very important. This is also why you have screens on all windows and vents.

The more you take care of the greenhouse and its surroundings, the easier it becomes to keep the pests away. This chapter provides an overview of greenhouse pests and diseases and how you can manage them. The chapter also provides insight into diseases and covers ways you can keep your greenhouse safe from them.

There are several factors to consider for successful control of pests and diseases in greenhouses, and some of them include:

- Proper cultivation practices that minimize the chance of pests and diseases building up.
- Early detection and diagnosis to enable prompt and effective pest and disease control and eradication.
- The right choice of pesticides and fungicides.

Some greenhouse insects feed directly on plants and some also transmit diseases to plants. Pesticides can be an effective tool for managing greenhouse pests, but most are toxic to humans and can't be used if you are growing organically. As such, if you are going to use pesticides, even organic ones, always follow the appropriate safety guidelines.

Let's highlight some of the common greenhouse pests and diseases, then go over pest and disease control.

Some Common Greenhouse Pests

Aphids

Aphids are sucking insects that extract the plant's sap, and they are found on the stalks of or under the leaves of plants. They cluster in colonies on the leaves or stems of a plant. Disturbingly, aphids multiply quickly in greenhouses, and can put your entire greenhouse crop at risk if left unchecked.

Aphid infestation often happens when the door of a greenhouse is left open too long. They also get inside through other openings in the greenhouse.

Fungus Gnats

Fungus gnats are tiny pests that have long legs and wings that allow them to fly around quickly. The larva of this pest is as destructive as the adult of the species. When fungus gnats infect plants, they start to lose their vigor and begin to wilt.

The fungus gnat feeds on both the plant and the organic matter in the soil. This feeding habit means both your plant and soil are under threat from these pests. The larvae live in soil clusters. Fungus gnats are often a result of overwatering.

Cutworms and Caterpillars

Caterpillars are the immature state of moths, and they chew on the leaves, fruits, and stems of numerous plants. A caterpillar infestation starts when moths get into the greenhouse through the ventilators. They also get in though infested plants that are brought into the greenhouse.

Cutworms are a threat to younger plants as they hide in the soil during the day and feed on the plants at night. There are also other forms of caterpillars such as the cabbage looper that feeds on lettuce. You can distinguish it by its pale green color and three looping movements. To monitor your greenhouse for these insects, look for cut plants or leaves that have large sections removed.

Mealybugs

These small soft-bodied bugs can ruin an entire plant by sucking the plant's sap. These insects are covered by a waxy secretion that protects them, even from some insecticides. Mealybugs can infest almost any part of any plant. As such, it affects a wide variety of greenhouse plants. Mealybugs also release honeydew secretions on leaves, so if you observe this on your leaves, you can tell when they are in your greenhouse.

Slugs and Snails

You will find more slugs and snails in your greenhouse when the humidity is high. Slugs are slimy animals that feed on the plant at night. They prefer cool, moist hiding places during the day. They eat leaves, flowers, and roots. They leave holes in the plant, and small seedlings are especially vulnerable to their attacks. If you find silvery, slimy trails in your greenhouse, then that signifies the presence of slugs and snails in your greenhouse.

Mites

Mites are very tiny insects that suck out the sap of a plant by piercing the plant's tissue. Despite their tiny size, they are one of the most dangerous and common greenhouse pests. These insects feed mostly on the undersides of leaves, which gives the upper side of the leaves a speckled appearance. When the infestation is severe the plants turn yellow, wilt, lose their vigor, and die. Roses are highly vulnerable to mites, as well as bamboo plants and ivy geraniums. Some bugs may start with one plant and quickly infest the whole greenhouse because the females can lay up to 200 eggs at a time in hot weather.

Most Common Greenhouse Diseases

Greenhouses are most commonly impacted by conditions caused by viruses, bacterial diseases or types of fungus.

Viruses

A virus is one of the worst problems because it is incurable. Viruses often present as a mosaic pattern on the leaves. Viruses are often brought into the greenhouse by thrips or aphids, which feed on the plants and infect them with the virus. When you find an infected plant, it should be removed immediately from the greenhouse and destroyed, preferably by burning.

Bacterial Diseases

Bacterial diseases include blight and they are also incurable. It is spread from plant to plant on clothing and tools. If you find that plants are getting slimy to the touch, remove them from the greenhouse and destroy them, again, preferably by burning.

Fungus

Fungal diseases such as powdery mildew are very common, and can be managed if you can detect them early. Root rot and botrytis are also common and manageable. Sanitation and low humidity are important ways to prevent fungal issues. If you have had an outbreak of powdery mildew, or any plant disease, all pots and tools and the walls of the greenhouse should be sanitized with a mild bleach solution.

Strategies for Pests and Disease Control

Know the Most Vulnerable Plants

Different plants react differently to various pests and diseases and their control measures. This is because plants do not all have the same vulnerabilities and defenses. Of course, all plants are vulnerable to diseases, but some are more vulnerable than others. Get to know the most sensitive plants in your greenhouse and pay closer attention to them, especially in seasons when they are most prone to attack. Additionally, get to know when plants are most vulnerable, for example when they are very young, and right after watering.

Prioritize Sanitation

Your first line of defense against insects and disease in your greenhouse is sanitation. You will have fewer issues with pests and diseases if you can maintain a clean and organized greenhouse. Sanitation isn't an activity to be done only when the greenhouse is messy. You should do it as part of your daily routine. Remember that the cleaner your greenhouse is, the less vulnerable it will be to pests and diseases.

Understand Your Biocontrol Agents

Biological controls help growers a lot, but they are usually only practical at a large scale. These bio-controls help growers by using insect predators to combat the impact of pests in their greenhouses. A good example of this is the use of ladybugs for aphid control.

To understand more about bio-controls, you've got to know the species you are trying to control, including its life cycle and natural predators.

Pesticides and Fungicides

There are a wide variety of pesticides and fungicides on the market. You can get chemical blends and there are organic products as well. Some insecticide products are targeted to specific insect pests, and others are just for general use. There are also many useful recipes for homemade pest and disease remedies. As your greenhouse grows and as you add more plants, you will have to increase your knowledge of pesticides and fungicides based on the kinds of plants you grow.

To maximize the effectiveness of insecticides and fungicides in protecting your greenhouse, don't wait until the issue escalates before taking action. Chemicals must be applied carefully and correctly for them to work. Not all of them are to be sprayed all around the greenhouse. Read the instructions and apply accordingly.

The timing for using pesticides and fungicides is also crucial as some pests will only die when you attack them at a particular time during their life cycle. Often, when insects are established in your greenhouse, you can only get rid of them if you attack them from the beginning and repeat treatment over several of their life cycles.

Additionally, do not use only one type of product repeatedly as insects may develop resistance to it, thus making your efforts ineffective. Try out new and useful brands and use pesticides and fungicides that belong to different chemical classes. Group the plant types that are always most infested and monitor them closely while keeping them away from the uninfected plants.

Find out what is available in your area, choose the product carefully and use with caution. You can learn more about pesticides and fungicides by reading about different products online, listening to experts on the subject and interacting with other growers.

Learn from Other Growers

Another great way of managing pests and diseases in your greenhouse is to learn from other growers who may have gone through this process and can share their knowledge with you. Always ask them questions about how they handled the challenge and get specific product recommendations from them as well.

Learning from experienced growers, especially those who live in your area, will help you make informed decisions on how to handle pests and diseases. Chances are, what you are going through with your greenhouse may be a challenge they have dealt with. Don't be shy to ask questions.

Have a Consistent Growing Environment

When you have a consistent growing environment, you are more likely to keep the greenhouse free from pests and disease. Consistency avoids fluctuations in water, heating, cooling, air flow and cleanliness. These fluctuations cause stress in the plants, which makes them vulnerable to attack by pests and diseases. Having the same routines will help you quickly detect problems.

You can work with a checklist to help you complete the same greenhouse tasks every day. Even if you get helpers, ensure that they do the same things at the same time every day. When you do this, everything runs smoothly, and the plants have the most stability.

Monitoring

One of the best ways of handling pests and disease control is early detection. By persistent monitoring, you will find problems early and be able to make faster decisions about what to do before the problem is out of control. Although you should observe your plants daily, make it a practice to monitor your greenhouse specifically for pests and disease weekly to ensure you spot plants that are compromised.

Pay close attention to plants that are close to ventilators, fans, and doors and inspect the plants in those areas every morning. These are the plants that are likely to be infected first as they are the closest to the points of entry.

You can also use mass trapping tools such as sticky tapes and cards that will trap insects when they get to or near the plants. If you monitor consistently, you will prevent a lot of pest infestations and diseases.

Essential Cultural Controls

Pests can get into your greenhouse on new plants, but some others may get in through open ventilators. You can protect your greenhouse from these pests through cultural controls such as:

- Find and remove infested plants from the greenhouse.
- Maintaining a weed-free greenhouse.
- Avoiding overwatering and high humidity.
- After every production cycle, clean the greenhouse thoroughly.
- Always scrutinize new plants before taking them into the greenhouse.

When you deal with pests and handle disease control effectively, your greenhouse will become an ideal environment for your plants to thrive. You will find that you have healthier plants, and this will directly result in bigger yields.

Consistency and diligence are the key to preventing and eradicating greenhouse pests and diseases. If you are not consistent, you may have great results for a little while and then struggle with ongoing problems. However, consistency makes it easier for you to establish a healthy routine and set yourself up for success.

When you have a healthy space, you will grow high yields all year round, which brings us to the next section about how to grow great returns throughout the year. What can you do to ensure your plant yields the best results, and how can you sustain it? Discover answers and more in the next chapter.

Chapter Twelve:
How to Grow Great Yields All Year Round

With a greenhouse, you have a unique opportunity to plant and get exceptional yields throughout the year. However, the fact that it is possible doesn't mean everyone experiences the same success. Some growers try so hard and still struggle to effectively grow crops because they haven't learned everything they need to know.

With every general topic you have learned thus far, there have been steps offered to guide you and to help you get it right. In this chapter, you will also learn the key steps to follow to maximize your experience and success in the greenhouse. You will gain insight into how best to achieve the highest yields in your greenhouse all year round.

Some growers complain about the inconsistencies they experience with the planting process. They have excellent yields one season and bad crops the next season. Such a variation in success can be very discouraging, and it can make the grower give up entirely.

However, this is not to say that there is a fool-proof way to have a challenge-free planting experience. Challenges are a reality of greenhouse gardening. Despite those challenges, there are ways to improve your chances of success. You have already learned a lot of them. This chapter offers even more insight into the steps that successful gardeners rely on to improve their yields and overall growing experience.

How to Achieve High Yields from Your Greenhouse

Start by Growing What You Love

When you are ready to plant your seeds, you will have a myriad of options to choose from. This can be overwhelming at first, so the natural way to focus your energy is to start growing what you love first. Of course, you can always broaden your scope to include other plants as time goes on.

Starting with what you love or enjoy most will help you get used to the process faster than anticipated. After perfecting the process with the crops that you like, you can take on more challenging plants and excel with them too. You can also start with vegetables you may have enjoyed in the past, or that are more expensive to buy than other vegetables. The whole idea as a beginner is to start with easier plants and gradually expand the varieties you grow when you have some experience.

For example, if you really like broccoli, you may have been reading a lot about broccoli, and you may now know a lot about it and want to try to grow it. Since you know how to grow it, its ideal temperature, soil type, nutrition, watering, pest control, etc. this means that planting broccoli will be easier for you. Research always helps, and it is always more interesting to learn about things you like! Once you've done a bit of research, get some hands-on experience by growing that item.

Make a Plan

Next, you have to have a plan for what you want to plant. By now you have likely decided if you will buy starter plants or plant seeds. This may be influenced by budget or availability. Knowing what you want to plant and how much room you have is your starting point. Learn about the plant's growing habit, especially if you are starting from seed. If you have starter plants, you will not need this information about seeds right now, but you may need it later.

All seeds are NOT the same. If you are going to plant several types of seeds, make sure you know the specific requirements for each of them and work towards using those specifications.

Then create a planting plan that details when you will plant the seeds, when their different growing milestones should be anticipated, how you will monitor and groom them, and any special needs they may have between planting and harvest time.

Planning helps you identify what you must do to get exceptional yields and keeps you focused on it. When you don't plan, it becomes easy for you to assume that everything will get done, but the truth is, you are likely to forget some things, or put them off. You need to work diligently and according to a plan to ensure that all aspects of the planting process are productive.

Create the Perfect Growing Home

Ensure that your seeds are planted in healthy and fertile soil, since it will be home for them until they grow to full size and get harvested. Once again, check the soil viability by checking temperature, getting rid of pests around the soil area, and ensuring the soil has been properly prepared.

This means that before the seeds get put into the soil, you may have to make some changes to the temperature and humidity inside the greenhouse, and you should water the soil thoroughly. Just like you make your new house comfortable and safe for yourself, you need to ensure your greenhouse is comfortable and safe for your plants. This is the new home for them, and ensuring it is as perfect as possible will ensure the best yields.

Test Your Seeds

Before planting your seeds, you might want to test them to be sure that they will germinate when they get into the soil. This testing process is crucial especially if you are using old seeds. If you buy the seeds from a store, check the date on the package to see how fresh they are. Fresh seeds have a very high germination rate, and the germination rate decreases as the seeds get older. Use the best quality seeds you can. The seed germination test is straightforward and has only six steps.

Step One: Get All Materials

You will need:

- Ten seeds of all the types you are testing
- One or more Ziploc bags
- A few paper towels
- Permanent marker to label the Ziploc bags

Step Two: Wet the Paper Towels

Now dampen the paper towels and spread them on the counter.

Step Three: Place the Seeds

Put the seeds on the paper towel and space them out so they don't touch. Do not mix seeds. For example, put all tomato seeds on one paper towel, and put another kind of seed on another paper towel.

Step Four: Seal Seeds in Plastic Bags

Roll the seeds inside the paper towel and press it gently to make sure the seeds firmly touch the paper towel. Place the paper towel wrapped seeds inside the Ziploc bag and seal it. If you are going to test multiple types of seeds, repeat the process and write the plant type on the bag with the permanent marker.

Step Five: Wait for Germination

Put the sealed bags in a warm spot in your house and wait to see if they sprout. Be patient. Some seeds take only a few days to sprout, but some take up to 10 days or more.

Step Six: Check the Seeds for Germination

Every few days check the seeds for germination by carefully unrolling the paper towel. If they haven't sprouted, roll them back up, put them back in the bag and tuck them back into their warm spot. When you open the towels and you see the seeds have germinated, count the number that have sprouted and multiply that number by ten; this will give you the percentage of germination.

For example, if 6 of the ten tomato seeds sprout, then it means you have a 60% chance of germination when you plant those seeds. The testing process is crucial because it prepares you for what to expect from the seeds and lets you know how much space to allocate to that group of seeds.

Planting

After testing the seeds or acquiring your starter plants, you can then plant them, and this is an easy task to complete. Simply place the seeds or plants into little holes in the ground, in the pots, grow bags or raised beds. After putting them in the holes, cover them with more soil. If you are planting seeds, check the packet for additional instructions.

Then place your water dripper by the plants so the plant can get its first taste of water. You don't want to flood the seeds, so don't overwater at this stage. Now you can put into practice all you've learned about watering, temperature, etc. This is the time to put all those lessons to work by ensuring that the plant has the best chance of success. Remember that if you are using a pot, then it will need more water than if you are planting directly into the soil.

Stringing or Supports

If the crops you plant will grow taller as time goes on, then you have to string them up or provide other supports. Stringing or stakes support the plants as they grow. Every plant should have its own string or stake, which guards it against growing into nearby plants or falling over.

In some greenhouses, the growers may not use strings or stakes; they may use some other creative tools to separate the plants and support them as they grow. You have to keep taller plants apart so they can have enough air flow between them. When taller plants have no boundaries, they become too difficult to manage, and their ability to grow well is affected.

Plants like peppers, tomatoes, and beans all grow tall, and they need supports. Ensure that they don't fall over or are not pressed against other plants.

Check Your Plants Until Harvest

Keep an eye on your plants as they grow, and watch out for changes, growth, and signs of any problems. The fact that you got the initial planting process right doesn't mean you should leave the plants and just hope that they grow. Remember all you have learned about pests and disease control. Monitor your plants every morning when you water. Soon you will see them sprout and open up into leaves, stems, roots, fruits, and flowers.

Watching plants grow in a greenhouse is such a fulfilling experience. At this point, you should know that all the plants you planted may grow and yield at different times even though you planted them at the same time.

Monitoring is also crucial for exceptional yields because it helps eliminate threats that may try to kill the plants. If you can catch a bug or mildew problem early, you will have a better chance of your plants making it to harvest.

Every plant has its growth duration and estimated harvest time, and you should know this information for every plant in your greenhouse. As the plant gets closer to harvest time, you should see all the signs of maturity and know that it will soon be time to harvest the fruits of your labor.

When the fruits and vegetables are ripe and ready, hand-pick them immediately. If some fruits are not yet mature, leave them for a while and come back later to pick them. Wash your harvested food with water and enjoy your yields!

Organic Fertilization

Just like plants need water, they also need food. A good quality soil will have lots of nutrients in it, but as the plants grow, they will use up the nutrients that are available. For this reason, you may need to enhance the soil with fertilizer. Fertilizers can be essential to success. The focus here is not on chemical fertilizers, but on the viability of organic fertilizers. Chemical fertilizers can cause harm to your greenhouse plants and to you if they are incorrectly used.

This is why you are advised to focus more on organic fertilizers that are natural and harmless to your soil and the plants. The organic fertilization process will help you plant and grow crops safely while giving them the boost they need to thrive in your greenhouse. When you go fertilizer shopping, insist on organic brands. If you don't trust the products available at the store, you can create your own organic fertilizer if you have the supplies available.

There are tons of resources online that you can use to learn about creating organic fertilizers suitable for all soil and crop types.

The natural process may be a lot of work, but it is worth it as it will help your plants grow healthy and have the best yields.

Consistency Counts

As you have already learned, when it comes to planting and growing impressive crops, consistency matters. Always strive to provide a consistent growing environment for your plants. If you try a particular planting style and it worked for you, why don't you use it again with the same plants? By repeating a successful planting trick, you will likely achieve the same results consistently without fail. Of course, all the conditions have to be the same, including the same type of soil, temperature, timing, etc.

To use this rule of consistency, you have to be very observant when planting, as this will help you know what you did so that you can achieve the same results. Consistency works when you plant the same crops over and over again.

For example, if you always plant tomatoes, after your first few tries at planting and getting good vegetables during harvest, you will know what to do the next time you plant. But if you have never planted cucumber before, you may have to take time to learn how it works before you can achieve a good harvest. Similarly, if you have a crop failure, try to understand why it failed and avoid doing the same things next time. Keep working at it and be consistent. This is the surest way of getting exceptional yields.

The planting process itself is never the same for all plants in your greenhouse. Sometimes, you will have it easy, and other times you will be required to work extra hard, especially when the weather becomes a challenge. The best way to consistently enjoy yields is to keep on trying because the more you try, the easier it becomes for you.

Most of the experienced and talented growers gained most of their knowledge by making mistakes and trying again and remaining consistent in their efforts even in very challenging times. Don't give up!

In a previous chapter, we talked about cleaning your greenhouse because it is a crucial step to take when trying to combat pests and diseases. In the next chapter we will elaborate on the best cleaning techniques to use for your greenhouse.

Chapter Thirteen:
The Best Cleaning Methods for Greenhouses

By now, you already have an idea as to why cleaning your greenhouse is important. We are going to elaborate on the concept because some aspects of the subject matter must be reiterated. A clean greenhouse will significantly boost plant production, and when your planting space is clean, you can keep pests and diseases away.

However, it is not enough to just clean the greenhouse like you would clean your home. There are specific steps to take to optimize the sanitation of your greenhouse. We will unravel all of these in this chapter. You will learn crucial lessons about how to best clean your greenhouse and how often you should do it.

When cleaning your greenhouse, you must recognize that you are not only getting rid of dirt that you can see, but pests and diseases that you can't see that could infect the plants. Unlike your conventional cleaning processes, greenhouse cleaning requires more attention because if one part of the greenhouse is not clean, that could become the breeding ground for bacteria that spreads to other plants.

Below you will find answers to the common questions about how best to clean your greenhouse.

Why Should I Clean My Greenhouse in a Certain Way?

When you clean the right way, you can get rid of all of these threats: pests, molds and diseases. Diligent cleaning while growing your crops will protect your plants from microbes and algae, which draw in gnats and flies into the greenhouse. If you don't clean the right way, your greenhouse will become susceptible to Pythium root rot, which accumulates at the root of plants, or powdery mildew which covers leaves. Both will spread quickly to other plants.

Some growers say they have pest-free periods, and then sometimes it gets bad. If those growers study their cleaning patterns, they will realize that the times they were pest-free were the times they were maintaining good cleanliness. Therefore, if you are keen on having healthy plants, regular cleaning is crucial.

Additionally, when you clean your greenhouse the right way for a long time, it becomes a part of your routine such that you no longer do it only when you want to plant, you do it at all times. Remember, diseases and pests cannot survive in a sanitized environment, and even if they manage to survive, you can easily spot, isolate, and eliminate them before they cause any damage.

How Often Should I Clean My Greenhouse?

Regular minor cleaning is required daily as it will help you keep the greenhouse neat and tidy, but the major cleaning tasks that are much more intense should happen each season and annually. It doesn't matter if you plant new crops that year or not, make it a date to clean your greenhouse thoroughly every year.

Annual cleaning helps keep the plants healthy and will also eliminate overwintering pests and diseases. You will also maintain your greenhouse structure for longer when you are consistent with such annual cleaning routines. If your greenhouse is mostly made out of wood, then you cannot afford to miss this yearly deep cleaning because wood deteriorates faster than metal, plastic or glass greenhouse structures.

Most pests and disease are drawn to humid environments, but when your environment is clean with your ventilators working to ensure cool airflow around the greenhouse, the pests and disease will have nowhere to grow.

How Can I Clean the Exterior of the Greenhouse?

By exterior of the greenhouse, we are referring to the exterior windows and coverings, which can be fun if you love cleaning. Get warm water, a sponge, and elbow grease! You will want the windows or plastic coverings to be clean to maximize sunlight for your crops.

If you are unable to reach higher parts of the windows, attach a broom to the sponge or a long stick and reach for the top sections. Clean all windows, even the ones that seem inconvenient to reach, such as the roof parts or at the back of the greenhouse. You may also use window cleaning agents for this cleaning process, but this is only allowed for the exterior parts, since you don't want to have chemicals dropping onto your plants.

Windows should be cleaned more than annually. You have to clean them regularly. They must be clean enough for sunlight to stream into the greenhouse.

How Can I Clean the Interior of My Greenhouse Effectively?

Start by removing everything inside the greenhouse, as this will make cleaning easier for you. Remove pots, plants, shelves, hoses, soil, and tools then turn off the electricity, so everything is off. Start sweeping, weed the plant beds, and get rid of all dead plants. Then wash the greenhouse by scrubbing the walls and all paths.

You might use some disinfectants for this process, and some of the most common ones you can use include chlorine bleach, hydrogen peroxide, sodium carbonate, etc. After cleaning, wash the cleaning tools with soapy water, and clean the things you took outside before bringing them back inside.

If some pots already have plants in them, then you can clean the exteriors of the pots. You can wash the greenhouse structure itself using an oxygen bleach solution as this will keep pests away. Only do this with the plants outside. To clean the greenhouse thoroughly, you will need a broom, rake, sponge, oxygen bleach solution, greenhouse disinfectant, and things like cloths, sponges or paper towels that you will need to keep the space clean.

The best time for annual cleaning of your greenhouse is in the warm spring season. You can also do it during sunny winter days but avoid exposing the plants to cold. Don't forget to clean your cleaning tools as well to avoid cross-contaminating your greenhouse with contaminated tools.

You can clean your greenhouse tools and materials with a sponge and soapy water by scrubbing them and drying them before taking them back to storage.

How Can I Clean My Irrigation Systems and Water Holding Tanks?

Some growers forget about cleaning their irrigation systems and solely focus on the greenhouse itself. If your irrigation system is dirty, you will be transferring germs and bacteria to your plants when you water them. To clean the irrigation system, you will have to use hot water to flush the pipes and soak the dripper heads in hot soapy water.

Scrub the holding tanks or reservoirs with a mild bleach mix as it will kill all the germs, algae, and insects like gnats hidden in them. If you have lots of pipes in the greenhouse, it will take time to clean and dry them and wash them in batches.

While cleaning the watering tools, remember to check the health of your water to ascertain if it is still good enough for the plants.

How Can I Maintain My Greenhouse Throughout the Year if I Am Busy?

If you are too busy to go through all the detailed processes previously mentioned, you can sweep the floor quickly and wipe all surfaces with a light bleach solution. You can also throw weeds away swiftly and clean the windows. If you are busy, you can still keep your greenhouse neat and keep pests away. You may not have as successful a yield as you want, but you can still enjoy a modest greenhouse gardening experience. Don't be afraid to ask for help from family or household members, friends or even neighbors who enjoy gardening. They might want to trade their help for a share of the produce, or just do it to be nice.

How Can I Get Rid of Mold in My Greenhouse Through Cleaning?

When mold accumulates in your greenhouse, it can become problematic for your plants. As such, you need to get rid of it, and cleaning can help you achieve that. Vinegar is a great ingredient that you can use for cleaning. Pour some vinegar into a spray bottle and spray it anywhere you see mold.

After a while, wipe away the vinegar with a clean cloth, mix one teaspoon of hydrogen peroxide with a cup of water, and then wipe it on the mold area with a wet cloth. The mold will not survive in the greenhouse afterward, and your planting space will be safer for future crop growth.

How Can I Further Disinfect My Greenhouse Effectively?

To disinfect the greenhouse, you can also use alcohol as a disinfectant to get rid of microbes accumulated inside the greenhouse. Alcohol doesn't last long and will have to be used often, so only use it for minor cleaning. Bleach is one of the most common disinfectants that can kill microbes. When you use bleach, make sure it is in a well-ventilated area for your own safety. Hydrogen peroxide is also useful, although it may be more expensive, and it is more appropriate for large scale greenhouses. Wear goggles anytime you use hydrogen peroxide, alcohol, bleach peroxide or other chemicals to clean.

How Can I Disinfect My Plants?

To disinfect your plants, you will have to clean the pots and areas where you plant them. Please do not use disinfectant on the plants themselves. You can take the plants outside and remove them from their pot if needed. Put them somewhere cool and work quickly. If it is hot out, make sure to water the roots of the plants frequently Then soak the container in a solution with one-part bleach and nine parts water for about 10 minutes.

Afterward, put the pots in a detergent and water solution to rinse, then allow them to dry out. While the pots are drying, wash the leaves of the plants gently with soapy water. After they dry, transfer the plants back to their pots, and you can put them back into the greenhouse to continue growing. This should only be done in extreme circumstances, as disrupting the plant in this way can cause it to fail. If you properly sterilize your containers before planting, and keep on top of things, you won't likely have to do this.

You now know how to clean your greenhouse intensely and thoroughly. Although cleaning is not the most glamorous part of your greenhouse gardening experience, it is vital to its success. In the final chapter, as a bonus, you will learn how to avoid typical beginner gardening mistakes.

Chapter Fourteen:
Greenhouse Gardening Mistakes to Avoid

Congratulations! You have arrived at the last and final chapter! You have shown that you have the diligence and dedication to approach gardening with an informed mindset.

We are going to finalize your learning experience by covering some of the top gardening mistakes you should avoid. You have learned a lot, but this is no guarantee. Even experienced growers still make mistakes and learn from them.

The mistakes you will find outlined below are common experiences for growers. By learning from their mistakes, you will be one step ahead and do the right things on your greenhouse journey.

If you have been reading with a serious expression on your face because you want to get things right with your greenhouse, it is time to relax. You don't need the serious expression for this chapter as you will be learning from the mistakes of others and then ending this experience on a high note.

Growing the Wrong Plants in the Wrong Temperature

A significant mistake made by growers is growing all kinds of plants at the same temperature without considering what works for the plant. Don't assume that every plant needs to be produced in an excessively warm atmosphere. If you do this, you will have plants that die from the heat.

Always learn the ideal temperature for every plant in your greenhouse before planting and try to plant things that like the same conditions.

Excessively Reducing Light

Sometimes in a bid to use the shading method when it gets too hot during sunny days, some growers ultimately reduce the light streaming into the greenhouse. A standard greenhouse covering should be 6 mm as this allows for 91% of light transmission into the planting space.

Your plants need sufficient sunlight to grow and produce excellent yields, as such excessively reducing the light will cause more harm than good. Find the right balance between heat shading and optimal light.

Watering: When It's Too Much or Not Enough

Even as you make sure your irrigation is top-notch and you are adhering to all watering rules, you need to ensure that you are not over watering or under watering the plants. Sometimes growers think they've done everything right and wonder why their plants still die. It could be because you misinterpreted the water needs of your plants.

To avoid this situation, you must always ascertain the right watering protocol for every plant in your greenhouse and monitor the watering system and your plants to ensure they are getting what they need.

Lack of Soil Management

Another mistake to avoid is poor soil management. The fact that your soil was healthy when you started your greenhouse doesn't mean it will stay the same months later. You've got to become dedicated to soil management right from the beginning, and especially as the season goes on.

Aside from the necessary steps of adding compost and fertilizer to the soil, it would also help if you use a blended soil mix that is rich in nutrients. Some of the combinations contain coconut fiber, worm castings and other organic nutrients that add value to the soil.

Growers Who Ignore the Growth of Fungus in Their Greenhouses

Warm and moist environments are a breeding ground for fungus. As such, if the humidity of your greenhouse is over 85%, then fungus will grow easily around and on the plants. If humidity is over 85%, it means that there is very little air circulation, and if there is also water on the leaves, you will likely get a fungus.

To avoid this mistake, please monitor the humidity level of the greenhouse regularly, keep the leaves dry, and observe for a build-up of fungus. If you see evidence of any fungal type diseases, implement sanitation protocols right away.

Lack of Proper Ventilation

Ventilation is a key aspect of successful greenhouse gardening. As such, when you don't ventilate your greenhouse enough, you will have issues. You can avoid these mistakes by calculating how much ventilation you will need. Divide the greenhouse floor space by five. What you get is 20% of your ventilation space. That is the minimum area that should be open for windows, rolled-up walls and vents. But you should know that opening a window doesn't mean the greenhouse is getting proper ventilation. The air needs to flow! You can control the airflow so that fresh air comes in from the bottom and warm air escapes from the roof vents.

When You Don't Consider the Nearby Trees

The wrong location is a mistake you must avoid. If the greenhouse is located in an area surrounded by trees, the trees will cast shadows on the structure, thus limiting the extent of sunlight the plants receive.

If you don't consider trees when choosing a greenhouse location, you will have a lot of debris and dried leaves around your greenhouse since they fall from the trees. Also, roots from nearby trees can grow under and into your greenhouse, thus eating up the nutrients meant for your plants.

Failure to Control the Temperature

Failure to control the temperature is one of the biggest mistakes greenhouse growers make. Some even forget that the temperature should be controlled. As mentioned in a previous chapter, the ideal temperature for a greenhouse should be 75-85 degrees F during the day and 60-75 degrees F at night.

If you are planting in the winter, then it should be 65-70 degrees F in the daytime and 45 degrees F at night. You cannot afford to leave the temperature of the greenhouse to chance because this will affect the crops immensely. If you can, get a digital thermostat to get accurate readings and then adjust accordingly.

Placing Grow Bags and Pots Directly on the Floor

This mistake is most commonly made by beginners who think it isn't a big deal to leave pots and bags on the floor. Growing containers and bags should be placed on garden stands or other raised surfaces like pallets or benches as this helps you optimize space, improves air flow and keeps crawling insects away.

Furthermore, when you use garden stands, it is easier for you to clean your greenhouse regularly without moving pots and bags around. Many insects hibernate under grow containers and pots placed on the floor during the day, and at night they attack the plants. This can be minimized and avoided when you use a raised gardening surface.

Effective Pest Management

Most gardeners fail to observe proper pest management practices, so they end up struggling with pests regularly and in the long-term. A significant reason for this mistake is because they don't pay close attention to the plants for early detection. Some growers wait until it is too late before taking action with pests, and by the time they take action, they cannot save the plants.

Daily observation is crucial in your greenhouse as any plant that gets infected can quickly spread the disease or pests if you don't isolate it. In greenhouses diseases spread quickly, and the only way to avoid this is through effective pest control.

Lack of Research

Unfortunately, some growers do not see this as a mistake, but it is a problem, especially if you are keen on succeeding with your greenhouse. When you don't do enough research, such as by failing to read books like this or learning through other means, you will be building your greenhouse based on preconceived notions that may be wrong.

Research is the first step all growers should take even before building the greenhouse, as this equips them with information that will help them succeed with the process. Imagine if you didn't read this book, and you went on to start the greenhouse process. There would be so many things you wouldn't understand, and this confusion would likely cost you a lot of losses.

Building Your Greenhouse Far Away from Your Home

You don't need to build your greenhouse in your backyard, but it does help to have it close by for monitoring and maintenance purposes. If your greenhouse is too far from your home when there is an emergency, you will not make it in time. In some cases, the problem might have escalated before you arrive. As such, if it is possible, make sure your greenhouse is close to your home. This will make it easier for you to pay attention to the plants and keep them safe long-term.

Starting Your Planting Season with Complex Crops

As a beginner, always start the planting season with easy plants that will help you garner experience and confidence as a grower. If you begin with crops that take a longer time to germinate, grow and harvest, or plants that you have to spend too much time on but have little yield, you might become easily discouraged. This mistake is one of the reasons why some people start the greenhouse process and then give up on it after a while. Start with common fruits, vegetables and flowers that can be easily grown, and as you get better, you can take on more difficult plants.

Having No Plan for the Greenhouse

Every project you invest time, money, and energy into should have the desired outcome, and this should be the same with your greenhouse. Why did you set it up in the first place? What do you want to achieve with it? When you harvest the crops, what will you do with them? Some gardeners do not have answers to the questions and challenges they face; hence they easily give up after facing a little problem.

Knowing what you want from the start helps you remain focused and gives you the courage to keep on trying even when you have to deal with natural forces such as the weather or pests. If you lack a goal or direction, you will do things only when you feel like doing them and not when it is really required of you.

Buying Fertilizers from Unaccredited Dealers

Numerous fertilizer outlets sell fertilizers, composts and other nutritional items for greenhouses, and it is easy for any grower to buy from any seller. If you are not mindful of who you buy from, you might end up with chemically infused nutritional feeds that will harm your plants. Don't take the store's word for it. Do your background check and ascertain if they sell organic nutritional supplements as well, and if they have a good reputation. If you fail to acquire quality products, you will consistently feed your plants substandard nutrients that will make them unhealthy.

Planting Too Much

Some growers feel that they have everything right, such as the location, soil texture, temperature, etc. and then they make a fundamental mistake. They suddenly feel the urge to fill up every space and plant things densely everywhere. They start to fill up every inch of the greenhouse with seeds and transplants, lettuce, tomatoes and flowers everywhere. This style of excessive planting violates the greenhouse spacing rules and could lead to plants suffocating.

Optimal spacing is required between your plants, and you must adhere to this principle at all times because when you don't, you make your plants vulnerable to the swift spread of diseases and pests. Airflow will be limited and during the hot season, the greenhouse will be very hot despite any ventilators in place. With limited air circulation, the plants will start to lose their vigor until they ultimately die. Ensure lots of air circulation in your greenhouse through optimal spacing.

Now you know how to start a greenhouse and succeed with it because you have been equipped with information. Remember that you can read this book all over again or read specific sections again when you need to. Yes, this is a beginner guide, but knowing the basics is where you need to start.

Before putting this book down, I urge you to read the concluding section, which contains a call-to-action prompt that will inspire you to start your greenhouse adventure now.

Thank you for reading!

Final Words

When you started this book, you embarked on a journey with little or no information about your dream to begin greenhouse gardening. Now, here you are, empowered with detailed concepts about starting your greenhouse. A good beginner's guide is a must-have source for learning the basics and for refreshing your memory about the fundamentals when you become an expert.

This book started with a fundamental and foundational section that offered comprehensive insight into the nature of greenhouses. The first chapter prepared you for the rest of your journey and provided insight into the factors to consider when you want to buy a greenhouse.

The construction process for a greenhouse was also outlined and we explored the difference between a greenhouse and a polytunnel hoop house. The cooling and heating systems of a greenhouse were a vital part of our discourse as well. You learned that proper regulation of the temperature is one of the keys to greenhouse gardening success.

Do you remember everything you learned about in the section on irrigation? If your greenhouse isn't connected to proper irrigation, then you may have challenges with your greenhouse. Growing seasons, cleaning processes, and how to get exceptional yields are also some of the vital considerations for greenhouse gardening. Now you also know how to handle disease and pest control and have reviewed a list of typical mistakes to avoid while working towards your greenhouse dreams.

With this brief recap of our journey together thus far, it is safe to say we have covered all aspects of greenhouse gardening for beginners. Getting to the end of this book is a moment that marks the end of your reading experience, but it signifies the start of your implementation process. What is the point of reading such an impactful and practical book without executing the ideas?

If you don't use what you have learned, you will never know how good it feels to set-up a greenhouse and enjoy the advantages it offers. While some other books are ideological, this book is 100% practical. This means that you will only get the full, true value of this book when you implement the ideas it contains.

You don't have to wait until you have access to all the required materials and tools and can make it perfect. If you need to, just start with what you have access to right now and gradually work towards doing more. The most important thing to do is to take action! A person who acts on what they know will achieve great success in their gardening.

Some of the best greenhouses you may have seen are owned by people who were beginners at some point too. They persisted and didn't relent in taking action towards their greenhouse gardening dream. The gradual steps you take with your greenhouse gardening will help you gain first-hand experience and grow in the process. This will create a ripple effect that will propel you into larger and more complex greenhouse projects with even bigger yields. Imagine being able to supply your family and friends with fresh produce all year round. That will be a fulfilling moment indeed!

The greenhouse gardening process is ever evolving and ongoing. The more you work on it, the better you become. The most essential step to take right after reading this book is to get started on your greenhouse gardening adventure.

Best wishes and happy gardening!

Made in the USA
Monee, IL
09 September 2020

41496526R10090